LIVING WITH THE UNDERWORLD

PETER BOLT

LIVING WITH THE UNDERWORLD

PETER BOLT

*To Grace, the gracious victim of poetic licence,
and to those of her generation seeking light in the darkness,
and rest in the chaos.*

Living with the Underworld
© Matthias Media 2007

Matthias Media
(St Matthias Press Ltd ACN 067 558 365)
PO Box 225
Kingsford NSW 2032
Australia
Telephone: (02) 9663 1478; international: +61-2-9663-1478
Facsimile: (02) 9663 3265; international: +61-2-9663-3265
Email: info@matthiasmedia.com.au
Internet: www.matthiasmedia.com.au

Matthias Media (USA)
Telephone: 724 498 1668; international: +1-724-498-1668
Facsimile: 724 498 1658; international: +1-724-498-1658
Email: sales@matthiasmedia.com
Internet: www.matthiasmedia.com

ISBN 978 1 921068 90 4

Cover design and typesetting by Lankshear Design Pty Ltd.

Contents

CHAPTER 1

Locating the Underworld

"*I* MIGHT WRITE SOMETHING about the underworld."

My university student seemed somewhat surprised at her father's announcement—and pleased. Was this a common interest emerging? As part of her course, she had greatly enjoyed her Film Studies unit on the gangster movie genre. What she didn't know about these films wasn't worth knowing (the exams were now over). If she wasn't a child of the Google age, she could probably list from memory the top gangster films of all time: *Goodfellas* (1990), *The Untouchables* (1987), *Once Upon a Time in America* (1984), *Casino* (1995), *Bugsy* (1991), *Donnie Brasco* (1997), *The Public Enemy* (1931), *A Bronx Tale* (1993), *White Heat* (1949), *Scarface* (1983), and—shocking because of its violence— *Miller's Crossing* (1990). Then, of course, there was *The Godfather* trilogy (1973-1990), which, in a strange case of life imitating art, apparently managed to reinvent the way the mafia spoke about themselves.

I must confess that, for a time there, I thought her

interest in the film-world of organized crime might see a few new pin-up boys on her bedroom wall (if she wasn't too old for that kind of thing): Al Pacino, Robert De Niro, perhaps even James Cagney. But things moved on to the sub-genres and spin-offs, whether Gangster Comedy—who will forget, *Analyze This* (1999), and who hasn't already forgotten *Analyze That* (2002)—or Gangsta films (apparently the spelling mistake is significant), with their associated Gangsta Rap and gangland subculture, or the ridiculous mingling of the two in the 'Englishman-as-a-try-hard-black-rapper', *Ali G Indahouse* (2002).

We could have gone on for many pleasant hours, as she chatted happily about the movies she had seen at uni (*and they call it study?* I thought). She spoke of the elements of society depicted by this genre and, in some cases, the elements of society it has created and encouraged, as she so helpfully handed over the piles of class readers, notes and textbooks, so I could follow in her footsteps through her underworld.

Don't get me wrong. I love being with my daughter, but sometimes her university education just seems to confuse me. You see, *her* underworld had nothing to do with my own.

Well, perhaps 'nothing to do with' is a little strong. Several years ago, as a part-time watcher of late-night television, I had stumbled across *The Sopranos*, the critically acclaimed drama that has recently concluded its sixth and final season. Whereas my family continued to do their thing for being Australian by watching *Home and Away* around dinner time, well after dark I began to mutate into an Italian-American mobster living in the suburbs of New Jersey. Some of my friends expressed a little surprise, if not concern, at my fascination with the world of Tony Soprano (and what a fine performance by actor James Gandalfini—the poster on my bedroom wall says it all). It wasn't my change of vocabulary ("forget about it"; "waddya gownna do?"; "he's gonna get whacked"), or even the accompanying hand movements, shoulder shrugs and facial gestures, that raised their eyebrows. But, they asked, what about all the violence, swearing, and depictions of sexual immorality?

"But here's the thing," I would say (or think), with both hands outstretched and palms upturned, shoulders shrugged forward and head turtle-like, in a pathetic attempt to imitate the great Tony Soprano himself, "it is so bewdifully made".

And it is. Tony is a mob boss, and yet he is such an ordinary guy. It is all done with such an everyday flavour— down-to-earth and realistic, thoroughly understandable. And it messes with your head.

One moment you are sympathetic, understanding this middle-aged man, empathizing with him in his troubles as he negotiates all the things of ordinary life: his bills, his possessions, keeping up with his teenage kids (their sport and schooling and spending, their changeable moods), his responsibilities at work, his responsibilities for other people, the pressures of enemies, the tensions brought by faithfulness to his friends, the pain of their betrayals, the struggles between his lusts and his loyalties, his dysfunctional family background, his own difficulties in loving his wife and his children, his twisted inner psychology, his depression, his anxieties, his fears and his downright panic, his desire to change what he can change, the rigidity of life-circumstances that just won't change, and, ultimately, the tragedy of his own inability to change himself—not even with the best of psychiatric help.

But then, suddenly, this sympathy rises up to bite you. For just when these late-night *Sopranos* watchers (I generalize for the sake of personal safety and reputation) are feeling that they are just like Tony, and he is just like them, Wham! (Often literally.) The outbursts of anger, the obstinacy, the pride, the arrogance, the mockery; the use and abuse of others for his own pleasure or perversion; the violence, the sexual immorality; his faithlessness to his wife, family, and friends; the brutal destruction of human lives and relationships; the perverse pleasure in the downfall of other human beings, the joy in manipulating personal power for personal selfish gain, and much more! It all comes from the same source. The Tony you love is the Tony you ought to hate. *The Sopranos* takes the gangster genre to new depths.

You get the feeling that Tony Soprano might have been one of the complex, mixed-up, thoroughly sinful people that Jesus was accused of hanging around with. "A glutton and a drunkard, a friend of sinners" his enemies called him.[1] When Jesus heard this accusation, I am positive he would have had a wry smile on his face. Although his meaning and theirs was very different, Jesus knew that he was indeed 'the friend of sinners'.

He also would have been able to locate the source of Tony's problem, and the source of all the world's problems—and it is a deep one: the human heart.[2] This 'beast within' is not really new to anyone; in our better moments we recognize that it is there. Our poets and songwriters have bewailed it, usually after they have experienced it—like Johnny Cash, who in his typically sparse and honest lyrics, writes about the monster inside:

The beast in me
Is caged by frail and fragile bars
Restless by day
And by night rants and rages at the stars
God help the beast in me

The beast in me
Has had to learn to live with pain
And how to shelter from the rain
And in the twinkling of an eye
Might have to be restrained
God help the beast in me
('The beast in me', *American Recordings*, 2002)

The Sopranos depicts this beast within. Did I say this series takes us to new depths? These 'new depths' are actually the same old depths. The depths of the human heart. It shows the underworld that lurks inside us all.

LADEN WITH ALL KINDS OF READING LISTS AND lecture notes, and listening to countless anecdotes and analyses of the various gangster movies and their connections, or lack of them, to the real world, I eventually managed to struggle out a couple of words: "Not *that* underworld!"

She stopped, looking rather stunned. Darn it—another connecting moment somehow shattered. Perhaps I should have lied and kept the conversation going for a couple of hours more.

I realized that my daughter and I had been dabbling

in two quite different realms, both described by the same word. And, to be honest, in a bit of underworld one-upmanship, I like to think of *my* underworld as the *real* underworld, the *classic* underworld, the one that has always been there, well before the gangsters took the word for their own.

But then, another thought. Why should I take responsibility for the lack of father-daughter connection? If *she* had taken another unit in her Film Studies course, perhaps we could have been on the same wavelength sooner. There are plenty of movies that show a spookier kind of underworld—the *classic* underworld. Movies about ghosts, demons, devils; witches and warlocks; magic and curses; black warriors from the shadows of death. Dark and dirty vampire movies eventually morphing into a form classy enough for Wesley Snipes in the *Blade* series (1998, 2002, 2004), and then, finally, when Selene the Vampire warrior adds sexuality, the entire genre is summed up in the single-word title that, by now, sounds very familiar: *Underworld* (2003), and, of course, its inevitable sequel, *Underworld: Evolution* (2006).

Perhaps this genre isn't worthy of its own university course, or, at least, one that would attract my daughter's interest. But the continued and abiding success of such films must show something about our continued fascination with this kind of underworld—the *classic* underworld. The long-running television series *Buffy the Vampire Slayer*, and its various spin-offs, explores and extends so many ancient views of the dark world which exists alongside our own, and makes viewers almost feel the mortal danger in which we human beings exist. The success of the children's fantasy series *Harry Potter*, still rolling out in print and in film, depicts a magical world view that has not simply been made up by its now very wealthy author. Magic and its demons, so familiar to many cultures ancient and modern, become even more glamorous in *Charmed*. The attraction of television mediums and ghost-whisperers to our television programmers is apparent—both in 'fantasy' and 'reality' shows. The blur between fantasy and reality 'crosses over' even further in the John Edwards phenomenon, in which Edwards communicates with those 'on the other side' for the sake of entertainment, first for pay TV, then mainstream TV, and then by way of an international travelling road-show. The magazines and newspapers can still dredge up enough psychics and ghost-busters from the real world, even if they regularly laugh at them as if they belong to the world of fantasy. But fantasy or reality, there is evidently enough interest in this stuff to keep selling magazines.

Perhaps a fascination with the world of organized crime can be understood as an expression of our real fear that something like this actually exists in Western society. Most of us suspect there is a world of organized crime that operates imperceptibly around us. In fact, we'd probably be laughed out of the lunch-room if we expressed an 'agnosticism' about that kind of underworld: "I am not sure whether the criminal underworld really does exist". But how do we explain the fascination with *this* kind of underworld, with the *classic* underworld of dark beings, demons, ghosts, and forces beyond our control? It seems strangely out of place in contemporary Western society. Didn't someone tell the film industry that we are all supposed to be secularized? Didn't the 18th-century Enlightenment make us stop believing in all that stuff—or was it the 19th-century scientific revolution? Or was it just the silent invasion of late 20th-century materialistic consumerism?

This abiding interest seems to be a throw-back to an age long gone. Since time began, human beings have believed that there was more to life than what they could touch, smell, taste, hear or see. There was this world, and there was another world. The two worlds were not distinct. There was traffic from one to the other. When we got all empirical and scientific, the thinkers of the modern world dismissed these ancient beliefs as the stuff of myths. Generally everyone went along with the 'experts'—at least, when others were around, and when the light was on. Now that we have arrived in a 'post-modern' world, it seems that many of us aren't too sure any more. What makes the 'experts' think that they know? How can anyone know? What if …?

Perhaps our movies are playing to deep, lurking fears we don't normally acknowledge, but which we occasionally tease in the comfortable darkness of the cinema complex. And in that darkness, perhaps we are brought face to face with a darkness that is not so pleasant. If the *X-files* told us that 'the Truth is out there', the swarms of TV shows and movies that have followed appear to voice the fear that the truth about the underworld may not always be so good. Perhaps, just perhaps, there is also something 'down there'. And if there is—what then?

"I MIGHT WRITE SOMETHING ABOUT THE UNDERWORLD."

Initially my daughter looked surprised. And I guess it is rather surprising for a born and bred, scientifically-trained Westerner with a handsome moustache (the moustache may be irrelevant) to turn his thoughts to the underworld.

But there is a very good reason for doing so. In practically every area of life, including the underworld, that 'friend of sinners' has got something for us. And it is no shallow solution to the complex problems of our world. It is something that touches profoundly on who we are and who we ought to be. It is something that deals with the underworld around us; the underworld below us; and even the underworld within us. It is something we all need to hear about, because he extends his invitation to us all.

There are three particular reasons why it is important to understand the underworld properly.

Firstly, the underworld is increasingly a part of the contemporary world. As I have suggested already, the underworld is poking its head into the movies we watch, the television shows inflicted upon us and our children, and the novels and newspapers we read. And all of this is an indication of the increasing fascination with the underworld amongst the people we rub shoulders with every day. Some are asking questions about the underworld; others have some fairly confused ideas about the underworld; but, most importantly, everyone knows that the underworld will take them one day, and—whether or not we will admit it—this prospect fills us with dread. And this dread eats away at our existence. It is important to understand the underworld properly, because our contemporary world desperately needs some good information.

Secondly, the underworld is increasingly a part of the contemporary Christian scene as well. The charismatic movement of the last thirty odd years has rightly reacted against the anti-miracle, anti-spiritual 'rationalism' of Western society by stressing the reality of the spiritual underworld. But the kind of interest in the underworld that they have encouraged has been (on the whole) unhealthy and misguided, and it certainly won't give the right help that our friends and neighbours need. It is important to understand the underworld properly, because the contemporary Christian scene desperately needs some correction in this area.

And finally, we need to understand the underworld properly because it keeps poking its way into the pages of the Bible. Since it is important for everyone—man, woman and child—to understand the message of the Bible, then it is important to understand the underworld. It is in the Bible that we will find the information needed to answer the questions of our contemporary world. It is also in the Bible that we will find the correction that is needed to make Christian answers much more helpful to those around us. It is important to understand the underworld properly, because this will help us understand the message of the Bible better, which will benefit everybody. If we understand the Bible better, we will better be able to understand the threat the underworld poses to us all, and this will help us to more compellingly hear the invitation that Jesus is extending to us all.

BEFORE WE TURN TO THE BIBLE TO SEEK ANSWERS about the underworld, we have to understand the very important distinction between the Bible's centre and the Bible's periphery; between its middle and its margins.

When it comes to the things that are central to the Bible's message, there is no doubt as to what it is saying. Its message about Jesus Christ is as clear as it could be. People may disagree with it, mock it or reject it, but, whatever they do, they cannot miss it. Whatever people's reaction to the message, they can still hear it, because the Bible's centre is clear. Take, for example, that famous Bible verse that attends so many sporting fixtures, and has even found a place in the crowd scenes on *The Simpsons*: John 3:16. The first half of this verse ("For God so loved the world, that he gave his only Son") is just as clear as the second half ("that whoever believes in him should not perish but have eternal life"). We may reject its message, but we cannot misunderstand its message. It may sound almost too good to be true, but it still comes across loud and clear. Part 1: God's love is declared by him giving his Son for this world. Part 2: Rather than perishing, those who believe in the Son will have eternal life.

That message at the middle of the Bible is so clearly and frequently proclaimed within its pages that it cannot be missed. The very frequency with which the message is told enables us to see it, hear it, and almost smell it, touch it and taste it, over and over again, from all kinds of angles. This all helps to bring crystal clarity to the Bible's centre.

It is a different situation, however, when we move further out from the Bible's centre. The Bible also contains things that are on the periphery, at the margins—in fact, sometimes almost off the edge! They are in the Bible because they have a part to play in the communication of the central message about God's love in Jesus Christ, but they only play a 'bit part'. Because they are at the margins, not the middle, the Bible never really lets us get a straight look at them. They never take centre-stage, but always remain on the dark edges of the stage. The camera never brings them into focus. They remain part of the shadowy background. They are certainly important, for they serve the purpose of allowing the central message to be seen more clearly. But they themselves remain rather blurry.

When we begin to talk about the underworld, this is an important distinction to remember. There is a centre, and there is a periphery. The margins serve the middle, not the other way around.

It's like watching a movie that is set in surroundings with which you are familiar. I love movies set in Sydney, my home town. I love them because I love my city. I love looking for the various sights that I know, identifying the streets, the buildings, the magnificent best-in-the-world scenery. I hope I might see someone I know in the background, or, truth be known, maybe even myself! But the trouble is, I find that I am so busy watching the background that I miss the story the movie is trying to tell me. I get so absorbed in the margins that I miss the middle. The questions that I ask about the background (What suburb are they in? Is that Short Street? Doesn't Ken the butcher have his shop just around the corner? Hey, is that me?) are all very much *my* questions, questions raised by my obsession with what is marginal to the story. I don't let the movie ask me *its* questions, which are, of course, the ones that will move me towards a true appreciation of the story being told. If I was going to be so obsessed with what was peripheral to the movie, I would have been better off spending my money to take one of those tourist buses around the city itself!

The underworld keeps poking through in the pages of the Bible, but it is never centre-stage. Because it never comes fully into focus, there is a lot that is not explained—a lot of questions not asked, and a lot of answers not given. It is as if we only understand the underworld in its proper place—that is, by its relation to the central message about Jesus. There is nothing wrong with asking questions, of course, but we should be aware that if our questions focus only on the underworld itself, we may never find the answers. Worse still, we may get so distracted by the underworld that we miss the central message about Jesus—and we really don't want to do that. We should ask our questions about the underworld by asking about how it is related to God's love shown to us in Jesus Christ. We should be asking how the underworld is related to everyone who believes in the Son being given eternal life rather than perishing. For, of course, if Jesus stops people from perishing, then he is specifically dealing with the underworld.

In what follows, we will start at the shadowy margins and work our way into the centre. We will first attempt to be descriptive, with successive chapters addressing different aspects of the underworld. Chapter 2 will examine underworld spaces—the geography of the underworld, or to use the more correct term, the 'cosmology' of the underworld. Chapter 3 will turn to underworld beings—the kind of creatures that might be associated with the various spaces. Chapter 4 will give special attention to the underworld master—the being the Bible calls, amongst other things, the devil. Chapter 5 will discuss what is, in a sense, the real terror of the underworld—the problem of death.

As we progress through these various aspects of the underworld, we will be moving from way out on the periphery closer and closer to the centre, which will allow more to be said at each stage of our journey. As we move from the spaces, through the beings, to the master, and then to death itself, we will move closer to the centre, and so more can be said, more questions answered, more help given.

Eventually, our journey through the underworld will take us to the centre, the message about God's love (Chapter 6). We will then begin to understand how our journey through the underworld exposes the wonderful grandeur and incredible significance of what Jesus Christ has done for us human beings (Chapter 7), and how because of his work we now live in a completely new relation to the underworld (Chapter 8).

The reason we can understand more as we move closer to the centre is, quite simply, because we are told more. The opposite is also true: when we are able to understand less, it is because we are told less. This raises the need for another preliminary observation before our journey can begin. Our journey through the underworld will be an *apocalyptic* journey.

Our movie makers have also kept this word alive for us, but unfortunately they have broadcast only one side of its meaning. Just like in the movie *Apocalypse Now*

(1979), an 'apocalypse' has come to mean a great disaster, the end of the world as we know it, the finishing *Bang!* of either our personal universe or the universe itself. This is not a wrong use of the word, and, in fact, it probably derives from the Bible—the last book of the New Testament describes such a cosmic end to this world, and although this book is usually known as *The Book of Revelation*, it also has an older name: *The Apocalypse.*

Although 'apocalypse' has come to be associated with a huge cosmic disaster, the word itself means an 'unveiling'. If there was something hidden on a stage behind a curtain, and the curtain was pulled open, then this would be 'an apocalypse', for the audience would now be able to see what was once a mystery to them. After you leave your magazine browsing and enter the doctor's inner sanctum, he could ask for an 'apocalypse' (that is, 'take off your shirt'). Although the thing on the stage (or on your chest) can now be seen, it is not, in itself, the apocalypse—the drawing back of the curtain (or the shirt) is the apocalypse that enables the object to be seen. The last book of the Bible certainly speaks of a great end-time judgement of the world, but that judgement is not the apocalypse. The apocalypse is the *unveiling* of God's heavenly perspective on this world—which include his plans for its judgement. These plans are not seen by the naked eye, or by ordinary empirical processes. The only way we can know of these divine plans is if they are revealed. To understand God's plans for judgement, we need an 'apocalypse', and this is what occurs in the book of Revelation.

Such an apocalypse or unveiling of the heavenly perspective on the world can only take place because of

Jesus Christ. The coming of Jesus Christ into this world has unveiled a view of reality that is unique and found only in the Christian Bible. It is God's view of the world. With the arrival of Jesus Christ, the curtain has been drawn back, and what was once shadowy and mysterious has now been made open and public. This is the clarity of the central message of the Bible. It is clear because Jesus Christ has made it clear. It has been revealed.

The closer we move towards that clear centre, the more light shines upon us and upon other things. The things about the underworld that are most at the periphery have a small shard of the light of Christ shining upon them, and so we can know less about them. The things about the underworld that are closer to the centre have more of the light of Christ illuminating them, and so we can know more about them. Our journey through the underworld must be an apocalyptic journey, for we can only know what has been unveiled, and what has been unveiled has only been revealed because of the arrival of Jesus Christ.

If you think about it, it has to be this way. If we are to understand anything about the underworld, it has to be unveiled to us. The old Aussie cliché is that we can't know if there's an afterlife because 'no-one has come back to tell us'. This is right, isn't it? If an afterlife exists, how would you know about it? One way would be to go there yourself, and, of course, on the standard theory, we will all take this journey eventually. But that might be too late—rather like arriving in a foreign country with six metres of snow on the ground and only your summer clothes in the suitcase. It is a little too late to make better preparations, for you are already there. The other way of knowing about the underworld would be to have someone else tell you about it. This is where our old Aussie cliché has missed an important piece of information: we *can* know about the underworld, because Jesus Christ *has*, in fact, come back to tell us. Our journey must be an apocalyptic journey, because if we are to know anything, we need to listen to the only one who knows. We won't understand the murky margins by looking at the murky margins. We will understand something of the margins by asking how they help us to understand the centre.

The coming of Jesus Christ into this world caused the veil to be drawn back on reality. Through hearing his message, we can now understand this world from God's heavenly perspective. As we understand this world and our place in it from this 'big picture perspective', then we can understand a little more about the underworld. And as we understand the underworld, we will understand more about the greatest victory the world has ever seen, the victory of Jesus Christ. At that point, our journey to the margins will have brought us back to the middle, to find once again the same message that so many sporting crowds are reminded of. Part 1: God's love is demonstrated in him giving his Son to this world. But there is more. Part 2: Everyone who believes in the Son will have eternal life. That is, they will no longer perish as yet more sad victims of the underworld.

CHAPTER 2

Underworld Spaces

*W*HERE?

It is a word that asks for a position, a space. When we think about the underworld, we still ask the 'where' question. The television medium addresses spirits with a *spatial* position, 'on the other side'. Certain spaces are believed to be haunted. The little child after his father's funeral asks, "Mummy, *where* has daddy gone?" After a fit of rage, someone asks, "*Where* did that come from?" In a world of inexplicable evil, we ask, "*Where* can I be safe?" In our world, we exist in places, locations and spaces. It is no surprise that we also think and talk about the underworld in terms of its spaces.

"Where are we?" can also be an indicator that we are lost, and have found ourselves in a place that we would rather not be. While giving me a tour of Chicago, a friend accidentally took a wrong turn. He was normally full of life and a man of many words. With this wrong turn, a deafening silence descended on the car. Startled at this unusual occurrence, I looked at him, and he even seemed to have become rather pale.

"Sup?", I asked him, perhaps subconsciously breaking out my *Soprano*-speak in an endeavour to fit in with all the dudes who seemed to be milling on the streets around us.

"We shouldn't be in this area", he whispered. "I better find a way outta here." Remembering Sherman McCoy, Tom Hanks's character in *The Bonfire of the Vanities* (1990), whose life unravelled after a similar wrong turn, I made a mental note about checking out the credentials of future friends-*cum*-tour guides.

Chicago. Yes, I know: the scene of previous gangster glory days. Although my friend was concerned about our present predicament amongst the brothers, I guess there were probably other places in the city that I would be nervous about stumbling across, even if for different reasons. Those in the know could no doubt tell me which clubs and restaurants I really shouldn't be in because of their criminal underworld connections. For an Australian who has only learned about the USA from the movies, I would probably be suspicious of many a venue in Chicago, or New York, or Miami, or Vegas, and now especially—since my late night television discoveries—New Jersey. Underworld types frequent certain places, they inhabit certain spaces, and although we might be oblivious most of the time, those spaces are all around us. Of course, as a watcher of *The Sopranos*, I know that this is how it all works. The underworld needs a legitimate business front, and so clubs, restaurants and other such venues can become its home ground. Even in my home town of Sydney, there are night-spots a parent might warn their newly adult children against, because of a suspected connection with organized crime. I well remember a friend who used to be on the force giving me a policeman's-eye view of some of the pubs and clubs that, until then, been innocent and neutral venues for me. Suddenly I felt naïve, an innocent abroad. My nice, law-abiding world had been invaded by the underworld. Call me paranoid, but I have never been able to relax in a restaurant since.

When we talk about a *Sopranos* kind of underworld, we are really describing a network of people. Although the word 'underworld' sounds like it is labelling a piece of geography, a 'somewhere', we all recognize that it is a metaphor. But just because we use a metaphor ('underworld') doesn't mean that we are not talking about a reality. The network of criminal people we call the 'underworld' really does exist—it's just that unless you are actually part of it, you won't really be able to describe its reality in detail. The metaphor enables us to speak about the reality, even if we can't say much about its details. (This is what metaphors usually do—they enable us to describe or illumine something via a vivid comparison. So when Jesus said "I am the bread of life", even though he was not claiming actually to be a loaf of bread, or even to share most of the characteristics of bread, he was saying something very real and true about himself. A metaphor is a way of describing something *in terms of something else*.)

When we speak of criminal activity using the metaphor of the 'underworld' we do so because this 'world' of crime tends to go on beneath the surface of normal society. At least in a properly ordered society, crime is not the mainstream. It operates 'under' the normal world, in places that are not normally seen. We need an 'apocalypse' to know where they are. And this unseen world corrupts and perverts and damages the society that 'decent people' seek to maintain and promote for the good of all. There is an inbuilt perversity about this kind of underworld; there is a darkness there, and the darkness arouses our fear.

Perhaps we also use the metaphor 'underworld' for secret criminal activity because it taps into older, darker, deeper fears. When the people of the ancient world spoke of an 'underworld', they were also using a metaphor. They believed in a dark, inexplicable world that could not be truly described by someone who had not been there. This reality could, however, be talked about by using metaphor, for such talk spoke of a world 'below' our own; a dark side, a world with its own dark beings and organization (of a kind). It too was normally unseen. An 'apocalypse' was needed to know what it was like, or where it was. Just as the *criminal* underworld exists 'below', but still damages human society, so too the murky *classic* underworld could affect and corrupt and influence human society for harm. Perhaps we use the same word today because today's criminal underworld evokes the same kind of fears.

These fears arise because of the knife-edge on which we all exist. Sometimes we 'demonize' those who do evil in our society, making them so like 'monsters' that they no longer appear to be human. This is a protective move, because if we make them into monsters, then we protect ourselves from the possibility that we might be like them. The *Sopranos* phenomenon doesn't let us do this. Our film-makers have done us a service here. Just like England's *Lock, Stock and Two Smoking Barrels* (1998),

or Australia's own *Two Hands* (1999) and then *Gettin'
Square* (2003), *The Sopranos* stocks the criminal
underworld with people who are just like us. It would be
much simpler if half the world wore black hats and the
other half white hats, but life is more complex than the
simplistic fantasy so often drawn by our moralists.
Ordinary people can so easily slide over into crime—as
victims or perpetrators. Ordinary people can be so easily
trapped into it, tricked into it, or just stumble and fall
into it. Often through weakness, or through some kind
of debt, they can be dragged in, and what begins on
friendly terms soon turns sour—like the gambler who
takes a loan from the kind-hearted Tony Soprano and
finds how quickly things turn nasty when he cannot pay.
Gradually his entire business and all that he owns is used
up in front of his eyes to service his debts—and then
he loses his marriage too. Who is at fault here? Tony is
clear: "Gambling is an illness". The underworld can
only do what it does because it exploits the weaknesses
that exist in the rest of us. The criminal underworld
around us points to the underworld within us all—
another metaphor, this time, for our dark inner reality.

When we use the 'underworld' metaphor for dark
realms of criminal activity going on just out of sight of
our ordinary society, it gains much of its fearful force
and power because it trades off the 'classic' view of the
underworld. But in the 'classic' kind of underworld, the
word was used more literally, for places and spaces, for
geography—or, perhaps more correctly, for 'cosmology'.

A COSMOLOGY IS A VIEW OF HOW THE UNIVERSE IS constructed and fitted together. In its oldest version, the classic cosmology had an underworld that was literally a place below the ground. As time went on, a *newer* classic underworld arose, which spoke of the underworld being in the realms above the ground, in the air, and in the heavens. These were all spaces to which people could go after they died. According to some thinkers, the air below the moon was full of souls, and so were the heavens above it. We will look at the kinds of beings in these spaces in Chapter 3, but the point for the present is that the underworld was both below us under the ground, and above us in the air and the heavens.

According to this ancient cosmology, then, the world in which we live was sandwiched between a world above and a world below. If you think about it, this 'triple-decker universe' didn't leave a whole lot of territory for the living to occupy. For those of us who live on the surface of the earth, the underworld is both below us and above us.

As soon as we bury our dead, we have a world 'below'. The corpse is placed in a grave under the surface of the earth. Very quickly the body decomposes, helped along by the worms, and so the grave is filled with rottenness and decay. It therefore makes sense that the underworld was regularly depicted as being a place of filth and rottenness. This was so well-known that Jesus could use it in one of his proverbial sayings, when he accused the hypocrites of being like beautifully white-washed tombs on the outside, but inside "full of dead people's bones and all uncleanness".[3] As we bury someone, the question is natural: what happens now? What happens to someone who was once so full of life? They have left a space in the world of the living, but what now for them? *Where* have they gone?

As we bury more people, it is also natural to ask what kind of society they might be joining. Human life in the world of the living is corporate, relational—what about in the world of the dead? As we stand at the graveside, representing those on 'this side', has the one we have just buried gone to join those 'on the other side'? And what is this 'world of the dead' like?

In the ancient cosmologies, the organization of the underworld could be quite elaborate. Various spaces were described—from the highest part of the underworld, the region which still gave some possibility of connection with the world of the living, down to the 'abyss', the deepest, darkest lowest possible region, from where there was no possible return. A journey across these vast underworld distances would reveal all kinds of dark scenery: murky rivers and swamps, pits of sulphur, lakes of fire, and everywhere the unrelenting filth of decay and rottenness.

But what if we start our journey a little earlier, not at the graveside, but at the death-bed. There, at the sad moment when our loved one comes to their end, they suddenly stop breathing. Where there is breath, there is life. When the breath goes, the life goes too. What happens at that moment?

In the ancient world, there was a close connection between a person's life-force or spirit and their breath— so much so that the original languages of the Bible (Hebrew and Greek) used the same word for both. The 'wind' from a person's mouth (breath) was evidence of the 'wind' within them (spirit) that animated their life. Breath is important at the beginning and end of life.

The newborn baby gives that massive scream as it sucks its first breath inwards—and it is alive! And then, at the deathbed, perhaps only with the infamous 'whimper', there is that final breath outwards, and our friend is alive no longer.

From such observations, it was thought that the spirit originally entered a person from the air around them, and when they died, that same air received their spirit back again. 'The air' was also a space. It was the realm between the earth and the moon. Above the moon, the starry heavens stretched even higher. Even though these realms are not 'under' us, gradually, because they were all viewed as 'afterlife' spaces, they became part of the underworld—the 'astral underworld' (from the Greek word *aster*, 'star').

Within this range of underworld spaces, there were places of punishment and pain, and places of reward and happiness. Punishment tended to be deep down below, and reward tended to be high up above. And we are here in the middle. With graves and the world of the dead below us, the air all around us, and the vast heavens above us, we human beings live on a very thin strip of territory indeed. We live on the knife-edge, surrounded by the underworld.

BOTH SIDES OF THE CLASSIC VIEW OF THE underworld poke through into the New Testament. It appears at the edges, and there is never enough of a 'front on' look to answer all our questions. But it is nevertheless there. In order to highlight the central message about Jesus, the 'classic underworld' keeps drifting in and out of focus, at the edges.

The message of Jesus encompasses a broad perspective on the ancient underworld spaces. The 'highest' place, heaven, is where God himself dwells, and the 'lowest' place is the 'abyss'—somewhere even demons are afraid to go.[4] Jesus spoke of descending "from above", and spoke of returning to heaven, to sit "at the right hand of Power".[5] Similarly, the apostle Paul spoke spatially of Jesus, when he said that he descended into the "lower parts of the earth", even the abyss, and ascended higher than the heavens.[6]

If the message of Jesus touches on the two extremes of the classic underworld, then it also touches on other points between. It is well known that Jesus died nailed to a cross. It is less well-known that some of the early Christians saw this kind of death as immensely significant because it was the only form of death that meant the person died 'in the air'. Jesus was buried in a grave, which took him to the 'underworld'. There are even some parts of the New Testament which may speak of him being with others in the underworld.[7] We find talk of fire, and lakes of sulphur, and the provision of cool water.[8] We hear of the realm of 'the air', and different levels and realms within the heavens.[9] There are terrible places of punishment and pain, and glorious places of reward and happiness.

All of this underworld cosmology, with its various spaces—whether the underworld below or the *astral* underworld above—is there on the margins of the New Testament. And it helps to illuminate the centre, where we find the message of the amazing love of God in sending his Son into this world, and in giving the gift of eternal life to anyone who believes.

How do we respond to these pictures at the margins? To someone who lives in 21st-century Western society, it may all seem very strange. The New Testament says that God wants every knee to bow to Jesus Christ "in heaven and on earth and under the earth".[10] Does this mean that Jesus and the New Testament writers see the world as a 'triple-decker universe', because they were part of the ancient world and this is how everyone thought about cosmology?

Historically, many Westerners have come to consider themselves beyond these kinds of primitive descriptions. After all, haven't we burrowed down into the earth, and haven't we sent ships into the heavens, and don't we regularly fly our aeroplanes through the air? And as we explore an ever-expanding universe, and find yet more worlds to conquer, we haven't accidentally walked into any underworld spaces, have we?

Leaving aside the question of whether your teenager's bedroom qualifies as an underworld space, when faced with such questions as these, some have been disillusioned with the entire message of the New Testament. If the New Testament is wrong about the 'triple-decker universe', then how can we trust it on anything else? If it condones such ancient (read: 'outmoded') views of the universe, if it allows the 'classic' underworld to poke through, then how can it possibly speak to our contemporary world of space-flight, deep mines and air travel?

But here I would caution such people against throwing the proverbial baby out with the proverbial bathwater.

In the first place, can we be sure that our visits to space, flights through the air, and journeys towards the centre of the earth are sufficient to prove a negative, such as: 'There are no such places as those referred to in the classic cosmology'? Can we be sure that we have the right kind of measuring device to detect these spaces? The story of the Sputnik astronauts who declared after a space mission that there was no God out there because they didn't see one always sounded rather naïve and misguided. We need to beware of the kind of arrogance that thinks human beings now know all that can be known about the universe. Perhaps we don't.

Secondly, it is not the case that the ancients were simply more gullible than we sophisticated moderns about such things. No doubt there were many people who thought the world was actually and literally structured as it was in the classic cosmologies. (And there are many people in our modern world who really do think the stars affect their destiny!) In the ancient world, those who practised or were influenced by the dark and murky world of magic may have been in this category. But there were also those who saw that the classic cosmology was more in the nature of metaphor— that is, a way of talking about reality which used picture language to convey something powerfully that could also be said in less dramatic fashion. Plutarch, the first/ second-century AD Greek philosopher, provides a good example here, following the precedent of his master, Plato. In the first half of his essay on *The Delay of the Divine Vengeances*, Plutarch uses a series of arguments to speak of divine punishment, and why it seems to be delayed. In the second half of the essay, he paints a picture of what we have been calling the 'classic underworld'. Plutarch uses the 'metaphor' to support the 'argument'. If an educated ancient thinker like Plutarch (and Plato before him) can be aware that he is talking about important concepts by utilizing metaphorical language, then it is very possible that another set of ancient writers, namely, those who wrote the New Testament, could have done the same.

Thirdly, if the 'classic underworld' uses metaphorical language to speak of large and important realities about God, the universe and everything, it becomes important to ask what are the realities being talked about in this way? When Jesus spoke in parables, it didn't really matter whether or not the details of the stories actually happened. The parables conveyed truth in a different way, a poetical, metaphorical way. So too with the ancient cosmology. I am an Australian. I once met a person in England who didn't believe in God because, "if God is 'up there', then what are you going to do in Australia?" For a while, I thought she was just joking around with this hick from 'down under', perhaps suggesting that 'up there' would be in England! But then it dawned on me. Somehow this poor person had been misled by the spatial language of God being 'up'—as if it ought to be taken literally.

At one stage of the progress of scientific thought, there was an attempt to be very strictly empirical and speak only of what could be proved by critical observation. 'What you can't show, you don't know.' But, as time has moved on, the role of imagination and vision, even within scientific theorizing and advances, has also been recognized. Some contemporary scientists have followed their ancient counterparts to propose 'alternative worlds' or universes or other dimensions, in order to pursue certain lines of enquiry. Now, it doesn't seem to be too difficult to think about God this way.

Let's make him hypothetical for a moment, just for the sake of the discussion. If there is a Creator God, and he is not part of the universe he has made, then perhaps he dwells in another dimension, the 'God dimension', or what has traditionally been called the spiritual realm, or—to use the spatial term—'in heaven'. No matter how bright we think we are, we do not have the kind of instruments needed to gain access to and measure this realm by empirical observation. We need to get to know him another way entirely.

This is why it is important to understand the New Testament's 'apocalyptic' message. The coming of Jesus Christ into this world has drawn back a curtain, so that a larger portion of reality can now be seen. As we understand more and more of the central message of the Bible about God's love for the world, and his gift of eternal life to all who believe in his Son, so we begin to view more from this bigger, 'apocalyptic' perspective. To convey this message, the New Testament draws in the ancient cosmology, using this language because it was so familiar—to themselves and their readers. Some of this audience saw the world in this way literally; others recognized that the cosmological language was a metaphor for other important aspects of reality. Both groups knew they were talking about something real, whatever they thought of the kind of language being used. And when the New Testament used the language of classic underworld spaces, it did so for a simple reason: to highlight and explain the central message about Jesus. Its 'apocalypse' was not an unveiling of the underworld itself, so that, finally and at last, all could see exactly how the underworld was *really* structured. No, the underworld language is at the margins, not in the middle; on the periphery, not in the centre. It is not the underworld that is unveiled, but what God has done for the world in Jesus Christ. And when we understand that central message, then we view life in this world in a completely different way. Even though we may live a knife-edge existence with the underworld all around us, the fear of that underworld and the slavery that it brings are now neutralized through Jesus Christ.

LIVING WITH THE UNDERWORLD AROUND US, WE ARE aware that the world is not all our own. There are spaces we call 'home', but there are plenty of spaces that are far from that description. The cosy feelings raised by home can be replaced by alarm and terror as we think of our home space being invaded or destroyed or somehow rendered unsafe. Even if we rarely experience the comfort and safety of 'home', we all understand the longing to relax, to rest easy, to have a space where we belong.

Unfortunately, our world often frustrates that deep longing. We are so often restless, even in spaces that we inhabit frequently, in spaces that ought to be 'home'.

To ask 'where?' is to ask for a spatial answer. Sometimes we ask the question because we are lost, or in a place we don't want to be. In the ancient world, the ever-present underworld spaces made the world a fearful place. What if we got lost, and stumbled across somewhere we didn't want to be, because it was a place we shouldn't be? An underworld place, a place for the dead, not the living. A magical place. A cursed place. A haunted place. An evil place.

Our cosmology may have changed, but we still find it pretty unpleasant to be lost, to be where we don't want to be. It is also quite clear that there are places that we don't want to be because they are also places we *shouldn't* be. There are places we call 'home', there are places that are far from home. We all have a deep need to find a place where we can be 'at home', where we can rest and belong and feel safe, especially in a world like ours which produces dislocation more often than not.

For a long time now, thinkers in the Western world have spoken of the profound 'alienation' that our societies have generated—a feeling that we don't belong. And it has only got worse in the postmodern world, where there is so much talk about 'community', but so much loneliness. The traffic jam symbolizes postmodern community—locked together with a load of people trying to get somewhere, with absolutely no meaningful interaction with anyone around you.

Where is 'home' in this kind of world? Surrounded by our version of the underworld spaces into which we don't want to fall, can we find a place of rest, a place to call home?

Sorry to be a bringer of bad tidings, but I have to say that it gets even worse. The Friend of Sinners taught that our real problem was the evil of the human heart.[11] Which is strange when you think about it. Quite often we speak of the 'heart' as the centre of our personality, the 'real me'. So if ever there was a space that ought to be a place of rest, surely it should be our heart, our very core, our inner being, our 'real me'. But the reality is so often different. Our hearts are restless too. In our alienated world, there is even a sense of alienation *from ourselves*. Even though we all have a deep longing for rest at the core of our being, we often realize that even in this 'space' inside us there lies a beast that needs to be tamed. And so we discover to our horror that not only is the underworld all around us, it also appears to be deep within us. There is also an underworld space *inside me*.

It is a good thing that the New Testament never brings its bad news without its good news following soon behind. In fact, it only brings the bad news so that the good news can be fully grasped. The good news of Jesus tells us that there is no need to fear the underworld below, above or within, because he has dealt with the underworld spaces once and for all time. There is no part of the universe that is not 'home' and safe and secure for his people. That is the amazing news at the centre of the New Testament, and after dabbling around in the underworld spaces it comes as a great relief—like that cool water that the ancient cosmologies sometimes included for some lucky underworld travellers!

But before we elaborate on the good news of Jesus, we need to press a little further through our underworld spaces and see what lives there. That's the thing about spaces—they usually get filled with something, or someone. After looking at the idea of underworld spaces, we now need to understand that those spaces could be filled with underworld beings. 'Where?' now becomes 'what?' or 'who?'.

CHAPTER 3

Underworld Beings

HEN WE MADE THE WRONG
turn in Chicago, it wasn't just the 'space' that caused my
friend to fear—it was the people who inhabited that space.
This turf was theirs, and we had invaded it. What if they
took our accidental arrival in their domain as a threat, as
if we had arrived to take over what once was theirs?

Okay, I thought, I wear a moustache so I could be
mistaken for a 1970s bikie, but on the other hand ... I
looked at my friend, now leaning forward over white
knuckles clenching the wheel, pale-faced, with beady
eyes under a sweating forehead. And, what's worse,
clean-shaven. Nah, not much of a threat there. They
won't think that we're moving in on their playground.

Then it dawned on me. My friend wasn't afraid
because he feared a defensive reprisal against some
would-be invaders in this newly provoked Chicago turf-
war. He was afraid because we had stumbled into *someone
else's* playground, and so *we* might become their
legitimate playthings. He was afraid because there were
people who inhabited this space, and because those

people might want to cause us some pain—of any variety they might choose. With this dawning realization, I began to mentally practise some witty banter in case I might need it ("Please don't hurt me!"), and my beady eyes joined my friend's searching eyes—only mine were searching this seedy suburb for the safe-haven of a local branch of the Australian Embassy.

When Meadow Soprano goes to college, she meets Finn, a nice boy from California, from an ordinary 'civilian' home. Gradually Finn realizes that not everything is ordinary about Meadow's family. Tony gets him a part-time job. But how come he doesn't have to do as much work as the other guys on the building site? And how come so many of Tony's colleagues just sit around all day, apparently watching the building supplies more than the building itself? And then, when Finn sees something that he shouldn't have seen, he begins to be afraid, very afraid. Finn's ordinary life has been changed by stumbling across the criminal underworld. As he accidentally passes into their space, so the people that inhabit that space begin to exert an influence on his life, and it is not the kind of influence his parents might have prayed for.

It is the same with the classic underworld. It was not simply the underworld spaces that aroused people's fear; it was the beings that inhabited those spaces. All kinds of spaces in the ordinary world might be inhabited by underworld beings, and to stumble across their turf might lead to fearful consequences.

When we begin to talk about the various underworld beings found in the classic pictures of the underworld, we find, once again, that these beings poke their way into the pages of the New Testament. They still inhabit the edges of the New Testament, but they are perhaps a little closer to the centre. Indeed, as soon as anyone picks up the Gospel of Matthew or Mark or Luke (not so much John), they are confronted with underworld beings rising up in opposition to Jesus as he goes about doing good. What is going on here? What are these 'unclean spirits', these 'demons', these troublers of humanity who oppose the 'friend of sinners'?

Once again, it is worth getting a feel for the classic underworld beings whose shadowy presence stalks the margins of the New Testament. If we become at least somewhat familiar with these beings at the margins, we will more clearly appreciate the glorious Being at its centre.

WE START THIS SECOND STAGE OF OUR UNDERWORLD journey at the same place as we started the first stage: at the edge of the grave.

Some history buffs and other odd types enjoy wandering through graveyards, but they don't represent the majority. For most people, graveyards reek of death. A graveyard is like a church building: the only time they have been in one was at the funeral of a friend or loved one, and so to be in this space brings back feelings of sadness and loss.

In the midst of these feelings of sadness, we meet the first kind of beings found in the underworld: corpses. On the edge of every living society we find its graves, and in those graves there are corpses. The ancient world had a euphemism for the grave: 'our eternal home'. Now *that* is downsizing! As the psalmist said, they may have owned country estates, or even whole countries, but a plot of ground small enough to hold a coffin is all they need for their eternal home.[12] As we bury the dead, we place a fellow human being into the underworld, with all its rottenness and decay, with all its 'dust to dust, ashes to ashes'. The underworld is a place of corpses.

What is this world of corpses like? How can it be described? The ancient world quite often spoke of life 'amongst the corpses' from the perspective of the corpse, to show how different it was from the world the corpse had just left. It was a world of darkness—they no longer dwelt in the light. It was a world of silence—they no longer heard the sound of conversation or laughter or love. It was a world of forgetting and being forgotten. It was a world of silence—as silent as the grave. It was a world in which the dead could no longer praise God. It was a world of no return.

Well, almost no return. Certain categories of people who died in exceptionally bad circumstances ran the risk of continuing to haunt small parts of the 'upper world' as ghosts—those who died 'suddenly and unprepared' (as the old Anglican Litany puts it). Those who died too young, or unmarried; those who were not properly buried, such as sailors lost at sea, or soldiers killed in battle on a far-flung battle field; or those who died in some horrible, violent death, especially those who were crucified! These restless spirits ran the risk of continuing to 'exist' in the world of the living, but it was not a desirable way to live. Better to die full of years, with your allotted span of life complete, surrounded by your friends and family, respectfully buried by those you love. Better to be 'at rest'.

There were other risks associated with being a ghost. Ancient magic operated by harnessing the power of these restless spirits. People in the modern world can't really understand the grip in which magic held people of the ancient world. Pliny, an intellectual from the middle of the first century (the century in which the New Testament was written), reckoned that he couldn't find anybody who wasn't afraid of being under the spell of 'curse tablets'.[13] These were typically sheets of lead, thrown into graves, and wells—places close to the underworld spaces—after being inscribed with curses directed at rivals in business, love, sport or whatever. The ghosts of the underworld were meant to fulfil the directions of the curse, which usually entailed inflicting all kinds of harm upon the victim's body and upon his or her family members. The magicians who sold the curse tablets must have done quite well out of the whole transaction. They also conveniently sold counter-charms that warded off the attacks of the curses from their victims! But both kinds of magic, whether on the attack or on the defensive, utilized the power of the underworld. The magician tried to gain control of ghosts, those restless spirits, and use them for his own ends.

With ghosts in the world, it was easy to be afraid of accidentally coming across them—perhaps at a crossroads (where ghosts were believed to dwell), or in a graveyard (where they were definitely thought to be found), or in some remote location which was the scene of the crime by which they were ghostified! What if you moved into a house that was haunted? Or what if a ghost moved into your home?

In a world where the local corner-store magician was selling curse tablets to your neighbour, people were not just afraid of accidentally coming across a ghost. What if a ghost was purposely sent to haunt you? In a world in the thrall of magic, ghost-power was forcefully enlisted and then directed at other people. If a child became ill, or a wife became unaffectionate, or went off with another man; if a business started to fail or if your lawyer in court suddenly got tongue-tied or ranted like an idiot (more than within the normally acceptable bounds of legal behaviour); if the chariot driver on whom you had bet your life savings (or just the grocery money) suddenly overturned the chariot around the corner and killed the horses—immediately in every case you would suspect that magic was involved. And if magic was afoot, then ghost-power was being directed against you. The powers of the underworld had been set loose, and they were baying at your heels.

But it was not only the external attacks from underworld beings that could evoke fear. It was also the contamination brought by their very presence. Ghosts came from the filthy, smelly, foul world of rottenness that is so well depicted by the *Ghostbusters* movies, or by Casper's revolting uncles. The rottenness of death was all over them. No wonder the Gospels' preferred term for them is 'unclean spirit'. The Greeks spoke of the 'miasma', the contamination of the underworld, and with ghosts around, the fear of contamination was strong. What if they invaded and befouled our space, our home, our city?

In ancient Rome and Athens, there were annual festivals which sought to drive the ghosts out of the city.[14] Ordinary homes had their rituals and observances to do the same. The tiles in the kitchen could be patterned with pictures of food, because ghosts were hungry and this was thought to fool them, so they did not harm the people. What a terrible way to live—afraid of ghosts contaminating your kitchen.

But the fear could go further. Ghosts were thought capable of invading bodies as well. This is the ultimate 'home invasion' or terrorist attack. Into our own bodies the underworld could come. How awful would that be— the loss of your own personal space and identity? We think of the man Jesus met who was so distorted by underworld beings that when he was asked to give his name he could no longer answer with just one: he had a legion of names.[15]

In the classic picture of the underworld, there were various beings in the underworld spaces, and some of these beings could somehow still influence life in this 'upper' world. This led to fear of attack from outside, but also fear of invasion from these beings, perhaps even invasion of your home, or even invasion of your own body.

Such fear lives on in many, many parts of our world, including Western countries. According to the surveys on www.religioustolerance.org, Americans are evenly divided as to whether ghosts exist or not. in 1999 it was line-ball: 48% of Americans surveyed said ghosts may exist and 47% that they definitely did not exist. By 2003, there was a slight change in the general figures, with 51% of the total and 58% of women granting that ghosts do exist. The age breakdown made it even more interesting. Whereas only 27% of those over 64 gave ghosts an existence, an enormous 65% of 25-29 year olds admitted to a belief in ghosts. Alongside mobile phones, iPods and the like, it seems that belief in ghosts is making a comeback!

Or take the example of Håkon Robertson in Norway, who in 2006 refused to tear down his condemned barn for fear of reprisals from underworld creatures that had taken up residence in the building. He told the Norwegian press that if he complied with the council's order to demolish, it would have serious consequences for his health and for his life. He was afraid. The creatures he was referring to were well-known from Norwegian folklore, but he wasn't simply giving a literary allusion, he had experience behind him. "A while back I removed the top of the building—and that is an experience I will not repeat."[16]

As this year began in my own civilized Australia, readers of *The Sydney Morning Herald*'s *Good Weekend* magazine were treated to a story about a bunch of present-day ghost hunters looking for the ghosts said to haunt Victoria's Cape Otway lighthouse.[17] Such people, of course, are usually the butt of the journalist's humour—the media doesn't seem to have any qualms about ridiculing those who have kindly granted them the privilege of their story. But no matter what the press might make of it, one thing cannot be ignored: there are many in our contemporary world who not only believe ghosts exist but are also afraid of them.

The ancient sources show some kind of 'organization' in the underworld, but there is no reason to think that this is an orderly kind of organization. It appears to be related to fear, threat and abuse. This comes out in the magical spells, which operate quite simply by fear. The magicians attempted to gain control of a higher, more forceful power, in order to threaten and therefore control a lesser underworld power. It all depended upon having the names of the spirits and the magical words of command. This was a dangerous business for the magician. In the early days, as the good news of Jesus was rapidly spreading across the ancient world, a bunch of exorcists were beaten up by the spirits they conjured,[18] and presumably this happened quite regularly. Many of the ancient spells also had a 'protective charm' attached to them to be used by the magicians to protect themselves in case they conjured the wrong spirit!

And just as the underworld spaces went in two directions—from the surface of the earth 'downwards' to the slimy filth below, and also 'upwards' to the air and the heavens—so the underworld beings were also found in both directions. The air was filled with spirits. The various spaces that could be described in the starry heavens each had their own associated beings. And just as the lesser spirits and ghosts could ruin the life of individuals, so too the higher powers of the heavenly spaces—the principalities and powers, the thrones and dominions and rulers, the *stoicheia*—could also interfere in the destiny of nations. The individual wasn't safe from these either, because these 'higher powers' were often the ones the magicians used to force the cowering lower powers to inflict their harm upon the living.

Is all this sounding increasingly like an episode of *Buffy* or *Charmed* or the next sequel of *Underworld*? It definitely doesn't sound like the news, or like the gossip magazines we catch up on when we are waiting for the doctor.

But think again. How was the influence of these underworld powers felt in a person's ordinary, daily life? Sickness, disease, bodily aches and pains, fevers and headaches; business troubles, financial difficulties, bankruptcy; forceful legal proceedings against you, incompetent counsel trying to defend you; a dramatic loss of a previously glorious sports team or racehorse; your partner no longer finding you sexually desirable, or being distracted from your relationship in their infatuations and affairs with a rival; your marital breakdowns; trouble with children, miscarriage, stillbirth, and loss of infants, toddlers, and children. Is this so different from the daily life of our world? The experience was very similar, even if most of us now attribute that experience to different causes.

These are the various beings that poke through at the edges of the New Testament. The term most commonly used for them is 'unclean spirits'. Unfortunately, some of our English Bibles insist on translating this term 'evil spirits'. Now it is certainly true that the New Testament *occasionally* uses this term,[19] and there is no doubt it is appropriate, for these spirits certainly bring evil to human life—they distort it, damage it and destroy it. Just think of the various people Jesus met in the Gospels, crying out with great need, distorted and damaged by these spirits. But despite the evil that they bring, these spirits are mostly called 'unclean spirits'. They are 'unclean' because they are from the underworld, bringing with them all of its uncleanness, its *miasma*, pollution, impurity, filth and corruption—the rottenness of the grave.

These spirits are also called *demons*, which is simply an English rendering of the original Greek word *daimon*. Across the years an elaborate picture of these beings has grown up around this term, so much so that they have often been explained as a *fourth* species of being in the universe—so that alongside God, his angels and human beings, there is this fourth class known as 'demons'. With this kind of thinking in the background, it comes as a surprise to most English-speakers that the Greek word *daimon* was regularly and frequently used to refer to the spirits of the dead. That's right: *daimon* was just another word for *ghost*.

People from non-Western countries don't find this so strange. They are used to dealing with spirits that we English speakers might call 'demons', but which they know to be associated with the dead. The ancestors live on. They need to be placated and cared for and consoled. Days in the calendar need to be set aside for performing certain rituals in their favour. They can be used by magicians to cause harm. On it goes, the ancient world in the present day, the 'classic underworld' in a different cultural guise.

And it is not just other cultures. The Western world is seeing a revival of interest in the beings of the afterlife and the underworld. These beings are now part of the menu offered to us on the silver and the small screens. Curse tablets written along the lines of those of the ancient world, but specially crafted to be directed at *your* rivals, can be purchased (for a couple of hundred bucks!) over the internet. Ghost-hunters, ghost-whisperers, mediums, spiritists, magicians ('black' and 'white'), rocks and crystals, secret names, protective charms and talismans, guiding spirits, past lives, ancestral presences, crossings over, and the list goes on and on. Underworld beings are not just something of the past or from other cultures; they are here, even in the Western world—the place from which science and modern thought is often said to have banished them. The underworld beings are undergoing a revival; they increasingly take their place below us, above us, amongst us, and all around us.

And so does the fear.

OKAY, BY NOW YOU HAVE REALIZED THAT I HAVE completely flipped out. Brought up in contemporary secular Australia, educated in our secular education system, scientifically educated with an almost dangerous commitment to empirical evidence-based research—and here I am talking about spooks!

But open your eyes, look around, and listen to what people are saying and watching and reading. As my interest in the underworld has grown, and I have started speaking about it, I am amazed at how often people have come up to me—sought me out even—to share their experiences. Many people have some 'spooky' event in their life—a place they will no longer go; a memory of a traumatic encounter with something inexplicable. Even though they have not often spoken to others of these events from fear of being labelled a loony, these happenings are part of their 'empirical evidence', and they have often affected their lives in some lasting way. So, to speak with Tony Soprano again, "Waddya gownna doo?" Deny it? Say it never happened? Explain it away?

As I hear such stories, the common factor seems to be fear. And also confusion. How do I understand what has happened to me? If I understand it, perhaps I will no longer be afraid.

According to first-century Pliny, a 'scientific' man who was rather sceptical about 'supernatural' things, everybody was afraid of the baneful influence of magic. That means they were afraid of underworld beings. In our contemporary world, in this 'underworld revival', the fear has also re-emerged. Perhaps it is sanitized somewhat. Like the ancients, who entered dark, silent public temples, we also enter dark, silent, public buildings, where we can have our fears aroused in the safety of others. And aroused they must be—Hollywood is making plenty of money out of them!

The ancient Greeks went to the theatre to undergo what was called 'catharsis'—that is, *cleansing*. As they watched the characters in some tragedy get embroiled with underworld beings, and the underworld beings exerting their influence on the living, the audience also watched the heroes deal with their own 'inner demons'. The hero always had some *hamartia*, some fatal flaw, some 'beast within' that led to their eventual downfall. To watch a tragedy was *cathartic*, because it brought the audience face to face with their own fears, and watching someone else's fears and weaknesses portrayed was meant somehow to cleanse them of their own.

Hamartia is the fatal, tragic flaw found even in the heroes, and found in us all. This is the same word the New Testament translates with the word 'sin'.

When we read the first three Gospels (Matthew, Mark and Luke), they give a 'slice-of-life' through the first-century world. Here we see the kind of people Jesus encountered and helped. Many of these people had been damaged or destroyed by underworld beings. Perhaps these beings had been inflicted upon them by their enemies buying a curse at the local corner store. We cannot be sure. When they find Jesus, he 'casts out' the spirits that have afflicted them. This kind of language implies that these people were 'possessed' by the underworld spirits. It is a terrible thing to think about, to have your own body, the last place of refuge, invaded by a harmful being. The 'fear of possession' is certainly exploited in movies such as *The Exorcist* (1973).

But, if possession is about unclean spirits being *in* people, the Gospels also speak of people being *in* unclean spirits.[20] Perhaps, therefore, the spatial language shouldn't be pressed too hard. Both expressions are simply trying to say that these people were extraordinarily influenced or affected by the underworld. No fuller explanation is given, and since we are dealing with questions that are on the margins of the New Testament message, we shouldn't expect one. What is clear, however, is that Jesus solved their problem. And he did so without much effort, simply with a word.

It is a fearful thing to think of being personally invaded, but there is something worse than 'possession'. Anyone with cancer can tell of the horrible moment when they heard their doctor voice the 'C' word. Life had been basically normal for a long time. Then they noticed something, perhaps something rather small. But then came the horror of hearing that word, usually echoing their own unspoken fears, and finding out that some kind of rottenness had been at work in their body for a long time—without them being aware of it. It is easy to be afraid of the 'dramatic' kind of underworld beings, but perhaps we should be more concerned about the things we are *not* afraid of; the slavery we don't even recognize.

Jesus was 'the friend of sinners'; the friend of those who were afflicted with *hamartia,* that fatal flaw that would eventually bring them to a tragic end. He taught about the biggest problem facing human beings. To a bunch of people worried about *miasma,* pollution and uncleanness, he said:

> " ... are you also without understanding? Do you not see that whatever goes into a person from outside cannot defile him, since it enters not his heart but his stomach, and is expelled? ... What comes out of a person is what defiles him. For from within, out of the heart of man, come evil thoughts, sexual immorality, theft, murder, adultery, coveting, wickedness, deceit, sensuality, envy, slander, pride, foolishness. All these evil things come from within, and they defile a person." (Mark 7:18-23)

Here is what we ought to be concerned about. Not possession by some underworld being, but already being 'possessed' by our own human heart, where our *hamartia* has taken root: the 'beast within'. Perhaps it is not always noticed, but it is there in the heart of us all.

There is an 'underworld being' within, that bubbles to the surface to corrupt and destroy life in this world. It will eventually take us to the underworld 'below'. The underworld beings may be all around us, but with a sinful heart, we have our own 'underworld being' to contend with. And it is this that will be the death of us.

People who have had an encounter with some inexplicable presence seem to seek understanding in order to reduce their fear. The New Testament addresses this fear by providing an even greater understanding. It may not provide the kind of front-on look at the underworld beings that the writers of *Buffy* would love to have. These beings remain on the margins, at the edge, in the shadows. The greater understanding comes from the apocalyptic unveiling of reality with the arrival of Jesus Christ in our world. He effortlessly dealt with the underworld beings he encountered in the lives of others. As we understand the central message of the New Testament about what Jesus has done for us, then there is no longer any need to fear the underworld beings. They can be safely pushed to the margins where they belong.

We may live a knife-edge existence, with the underworld spaces all around us. We may live with underworld beings also surrounding us. The darkness may press in upon us, with all its potential threats and fears. The air may be filled with all kinds of ghosts, souls and unclean spirits. But in that same air, once long ago, a special man died—in the midst of the air, with his hands outstretched to the world. It is there, in that moment, that we will find our true *catharsis.*

CHAPTER 4

The Underworld Master

*T*HERE IS ONE LAST underworld being that we need to take a look at. In these various underworld spaces, filled with various underworld beings, there is one who is portrayed as their prince. What is his role? And, remembering that we are looking at the edge to understand the centre, what does Jesus do about this prince?

There is no doubt that Tony is 'the Boss' of the Sopranos crime family. This family represents the criminal underworld, aka 'organized crime'. At the top of the pile in this organization is the boss, who is owed and demands respect. Sometimes this respect comes from good decisions, from looking after his men, from being good for the family. Other times it comes from old-fashioned fear and the use of raw muscle.

At the end of the fifth series, Tony is shot. He lies in a coma for the whole time between seasons (while I was enjoying Australia's summer), but eventually emerges from the coma in an okay sort of condition—not great, just okay. From that point, he is constantly mollycoddled by the women in his life, and his men start the gentle treatment as well. He realizes he is losing respect. One day he sits sizing up his men: who is the biggest? the strongest? He chooses a young, fit guy, with biceps the size of thighs. Suddenly, for no reason apparent to anyone else, Tony up and bashes the guy. But Tony knows why. This self-serving, arbitrary display of power has a very clear purpose: it wins back his respect. It shows everyone who is boss.

As boss, Tony exercises absolute power. If his underlings want to organize a new way of earning, he grants permission—and, of course, receives his share of the takings. He approves the territory that each of them works in. He gives his okay to the kind of activity, and the ways it is to be performed. And this is all backed up by his power over his men. His position as Boss contains the threat that it can be enforced if necessary; and those under him live in fear. If they step out of line—even if they can't really tell what they have done to provoke Tony's rage—his power will be unleashed in their direction, and that won't be pleasant. Such is the power of the boss in the criminal underworld.

It was the same in the classic underworld. There was Hades, of course, the 'god' of the underworld, whose name was often also used to describe the place over which he ruled. But then there was the 'prince of daimons'—perhaps Hades, perhaps another—who gave permission for the ghosts (daimons) to be released into the upper world.

When we turn to the New Testament, we find Jesus being accused of being in league with this 'prince of daimons'—as if Jesus was some kind of magician who had worked out how to threaten the underworld prince so as to gain some advantage for himself: "... by the prince of demons he casts out the demons".[21] But his enemies were mistaken. As his future resurrection from the dead would definitively show, Jesus had come to overthrow and replace this prince of demons.

The arrival of Jesus Christ brought an apocalyptic unveiling of reality that was startling in its effects and obvious to those who lived at the time. Even the most sceptical New Testament scholar admits that Jesus was known for his extraordinary ability to deal with the unclean spirits of the underworld. No-one in Jesus' time disputed his ability to do 'exorcisms'; they simply debated the source of his power. He said he did these things because he was sent by God the Creator (whom he called 'Father'). His enemies said he did such things because he was a magician, a sorcerer, utilizing the power of "Beelzebul, the Prince of daimons".

Jesus' arrival in this world unleashed a counter-reaction from the underworld because he had come to take on the one who had formerly been in charge. The unclean spirits rose up against him: "What have you to do with us, Jesus of Nazareth? Have you come to destroy us?"[22] Jesus was moving into their turf, mounting a challenge to the one who was their boss. And the reigning 'boss' was not happy.

WHEN WE BEGIN TO TAKE A LOOK AT THE MASTER of the underworld, we have begun to move closer to the centre of the New Testament. This master goes by many names: Satan, the devil, the enemy, the tester, the evil one, the adversary, Beelzebul. In our contemporary world, we have largely forgotten that a name actually meant something about the person wearing it. I cringe a little when parents call their newborn daughter Anake, since this was the Greek goddess of hard-hearted necessity —what does that say about the future 'stubborn streak' that might develop in the girl? (Apparently 'Annika' means something much nicer in Nordic.) Each of the names of the underworld master shows a significant aspect of the warped character and twisted activity of this so-called prince. He is 'the accuser' (Satan), 'the slanderer' (devil), the one who opposes God's good purposes (the enemy), the one who puts human beings under great pressure (the tester), the one who deceives them and leads them astray (the deceiver), the one who brings evil upon human beings (the evil one), the one who kills (the murderer from the beginning), the one who constantly stands against them and against their good (the adversary). Imagine living under the rule of such a leader!

If we examine the history of Western thought, we would be justified in speaking of 'the demise of the devil'. Perhaps in the medieval period, people gave far too much attention to this figure. In our day, we tend to have the opposite problem. Feminism is one indicator of the irrelevance with which the devil is treated. In the forty years or so in which the feminist cause has been championed strongly, there have been many and varied suggestions made to replace the masculine pronoun when referring to God. Why should God be pictured as a male? To my knowledge, however, in this same period absolutely no-one has objected to the devil being described as a 'he'. Now, the cynic may take this as an indication of what feminism thinks of the male of the species. The devil and men deserve each other! But it more likely indicates the current lack of concern about the devil to many of our contemporaries. Certainly in intellectual circles, or in science, or in the arena of politics, the devil would not be a topic that is discussed seriously too often, if at all. *He* would usually be placed in the realm of mythology or fantasy.

However, even in the West, interest in the devil has not completely disappeared. Every now and again we are made aware of those who call themselves Satanists. As with the criminal underworld, we all know or suspect that these people are there, but they usually exist in their own dark sub-culture and keep to themselves. Occasionally, however, their 'fantasy' becomes a shocking reality foisted upon the rest of society. Take, for example, the case of Manuela and Daniel Ruda, two Satanists who went on trial in Bochum, Germany, as recently as 2002 for the brutal slaying of their friend. Satan told them to.

These two were also self-styled vampires. Daniel originally met Manuela by placing an ad in a lonely hearts column: "Vampire seeks princess of darkness that hates everyone and everything". Manuela had first become involved with Satanists at the age of 16, when she ran away from home to England and Scotland. When she returned to Germany, she threw herself into the satanic scene and, for good measure, she had some teeth removed and replaced with animal fangs. After committing the brutal murder, the couple drank their victim's blood. Manuela stated, "We were empowered and alone". She described how disappointed she was that after the killing she did not turn into a vampire, "because as a vampire I would not have needed the streets".[23] When the 23- and 26-year-old were sent by the court to secure psychiatric institutions, most Westerners would have thought this appropriate. Surely you must be 'mad' not only to serve Satan in such anti-social and inhuman ways, but even to believe in him in the first place.

But if this were so, then the prisons and secure psychiatric institutions would be even fuller than they are. Just as belief in the existence of ghosts may be climbing (see last chapter), so also belief in the devil seems to have taken a turn upwards (or is that downwards?). According to the surveys on www.religioustolerance.org, whereas 62% of Americans surveyed in 1997 thought Satan was merely a symbol of evil, in 2003 68% said that he was real. In 2002, a newspaper poll showed that the ordinary Australian was more likely to believe in the devil than in God.

The devil has also been domesticated somewhat. Various practices traditionally associated with the devil have now entered the mainstream. Horoscopes and other occult practices, once regarded as satanic, now litter the popular magazines as a little bit of fun. Spells, both for good and evil, can be purchased on the internet. Witches strive to be recognized as offering a legitimate religion.

Not everyone treats the devil so neutrally, however. In some Christian circles, interest in the devil is climbing to almost medieval proportions. Over the last thirty years or so, some elements of the charismatic movement have revived the practice of exorcism. Sadly, this has led to a number of weird practices that are certainly not endorsed by the New Testament, and are actually discouraged.

One of the tragedies of recent decades is that many people have actually been killed in 'exorcisms' gone sadly wrong. These were not all 'Christian' exorcisms, since exorcisms are practised by various groups, from voodoo to the Falun Gong. But it is unfortunate—no, it's an abomination!—that some of these killings were done in the name of Christianity.

Anneliese Michel, whose story is told by the films *The Exorcism of Emily Rose* (2005) and *Requiem* (2006), was killed in Bavaria in 1976. Joan Vollmer died in 1994 in Victoria, Australia, beaten to death by her husband and his associates. Same story for Kyung-A Ha a year later in California, and Kyung Jae Chung the year after that, also in California. 1996 also saw two-year old Kira Canhoto drowned by water forced down her throat by her grandmother in an attempt to get rid of demons. In 1997 it was a mixture of ammonia and vinegar that was poured down the throat of a five-year-old in the Bronx. In 1998, in Sayville, New York, 17-year-old Charity Miranda was suffocated with a plastic bag by her mother and sister in a Cuban voodoo exorcism. In 2000, a three-year-old in New South Wales was drowned by his mother, again by pouring water down his throat in an attempt to get rid of demons. In 2001, in a similar effort to drive out demons, 37-year-old Joanna Lee was strangled in Auckland, and in 2002 in China, another child, nine years old, was choked to death by her mother, apparently a member of the Falun Gong. Then there was Terrance Cottrell Jr., an eight-year-old autistic child, asphyxiated in 2003. A six-year-old girl died after her back was broken in Atlanta, 2004. The next year saw the famous case of a Romanian Catholic nun dying after being hung on a cross as part of an exorcism.

Any practice that so regularly ends up in the loss of human life is far more likely to come from the one who is "a murderer from the beginning" than from the one who is "the Author of life".[24] And any practice that is valued by ancient and modern magic, voodoo and other non-Christian religions should be viewed as highly questionable by Christians. However, this has not prevented some sadly misguided Christians becoming involved in these sorts of practices—practices that should never be attempted (more on this in Chapter 7). Even if these cases are at the 'extreme' end, Christian bookstores continue to pump out numerous popular titles about the devil, and there are numerous Christian organizations and churches encouraging what is (wrongly) called 'spiritual warfare'.

Sometimes this over-fascination with the devil gives a completely wrong impression of the reality. There are Christian novels (racy, enjoyable, exciting novels—no wonder they are best-sellers) that seem to depict the battle between God and the devil as if it hung in the balance, an evenly pitched battle between forces of almost equal strength and power. This is certainly not the case at all. The apocalyptic unveiling of reality that occurred when Jesus arrived showed his effortless, decisive, lasting victory over the powers of evil. "The reason the Son of God appeared was to destroy the works of the devil",[25] and he did! And the only person who died in the process was Jesus himself!

WE HAVE BEEN RACING AHEAD SOMEWHAT. BEFORE we get to how the devil has been dealt with, we need to understand more about how he operates—this underworld prince with so many names, each speaking of his mission to deceive, damage and destroy human beings. Jesus said he was a liar and a murderer from the beginning.[26] That about sums up what he does. He lies to deceive, and once he has deceived, he kills. Most of us don't really want to be vampires or Satan-worshippers; most of us would prefer to be just ordinary human beings. What has this master of the underworld got to do with us? The answer is that we, too, are deceived in order to be killed.

Have you ever heard others saying, or found yourself saying, "The devil made me do it"? Or perhaps these days, people say, "I don't know what came over me", or "Where did that come from?" I guess these phrases are an attempt to explain a certain action as out of character for us, as something that appears to have been inspired 'from outside'—perhaps even 'from below'. It may even be an attempt to shift responsibility.

But perhaps blaming an outside influence is more often a 'cry for help'. Even though we don't usually reflect on its implications this deeply, when someone uses an expression like this it shows the terrible state that they have fallen into. They have been overtaken by evil. They have become aware that an evil power greater than themselves has taken them captive in some way.

We might feel sorry for such a person. But in our increasingly dysfunctional—and so increasingly moralistic —world, we are perhaps more likely to blame them for being so weak, and to congratulate ourselves that 'we are not like these other sinners' (as the Pharisee does in Luke 18). Thus we can call on people to stop doing the wrong thing, so that rightness and goodness will prevail. Moralism is so simple: everything is about behaviour, and change is so easy. It just involves stopping the wrong thing, and starting the right thing. What could be easier? And in this system, sympathy is deemed to be misguided. If someone is doing the wrong thing then they don't deserve sympathy, they need a good kick in the behind—or worse!

It is a pity that moralism has always been so rampant amongst people who say they are trying to live by the Bible. If Christians were to read the New Testament and grasp its central message, they could never join the moralists, and they would be the most sympathetic people this world has ever seen.

'The devil made me do it.' Isn't that one of the most awful tragedies that could befall a human being? Jesus spoke about our biggest problem being the problem of the human heart, the underworld within, taking us headlong into the underworld proper. The New Testament continues this theme on page after page. It certainly holds us responsible for our wrong choices. But it does not simply damn us for 'doing the wrong thing', and then call upon us to change direction. Instead it points to our great tragedy, the *hamartia* within, the fatal flaw that leads eventually to our ruin. It says that we are weak, helpless and lost. And being weak, helpless and lost, we have fallen prey to an evil power, so real that our modern world has to laugh at it, for fear of crying.

Moralists can't seem to cope with such words about weakness and fatal flaws. "Won't these words let people off the hook? Won't this let them wriggle out of their responsibility?" Moralists seek to redefine these words in terms of doing the wrong thing. Lost means 'in the grip of sin'; weak means 'not having enough moral fortitude'; helpless means 'for goodness sake, stop snivelling and get a grip!' But that is not the Bible's way of talking. To be weak is to be diminished in our capacity to change. To be helpless is to be unable to help ourselves. To be lost is exactly that, heading for destruction with no visible way of escape. When we understand the true depths of humanity's plight, the moralists' mere exhortations ('Don't be weak'; 'Help yourself'; 'Get un-lost') sound, well, to be truthful—monstrously inhuman.

Not so the glorious New Testament. When the New Testament speaks about the human condition, you can feel the sympathy, the fellow-feeling. For the central message of the New Testament is not a call for wrongly behaving people to start doing the right thing; it is a *promise* that God has freely given them a solution to the terrible state they have found themselves in. We may be sinners—that's for sure—but when God so loved the world, he sent us a 'friend of sinners' to provide a real solution.

As the French Christian philosopher Blaise Pascal put it, human beings were made to be the glory of the universe, but we have become the garbage (loosely translated!). The apocalyptic message of the New Testament folds back this piece of reality so we can see the terrible state of life in which we actually live. The gospel of Jesus is proclaimed to a lost world so that people might "escape from the snare of the devil", who has taken us captive to do his will.[27] We have been lied to and deceived; and all this has been made possible because of our weakness, our fatal flaw, our sin. We have fallen into slavery without realizing!

When Jesus was about thirty, he stepped out of the carpenter's shop and began the public work that God (whom he called 'my Father') had called him to do. Immediately, the boss of the underworld rose up against him. Even if everyone else was oblivious of what was going on, the prince of demons and his underworld forces certainly recognized the turf war that was about to begin. The devil called upon Jesus to bow down and worship him rather than the Father—something Jesus refused to do. As the story is told in Luke's Gospel, Satan took Jesus up on a very high mountain and showed him all the kingdoms of the earth and their glory. This was the carrot to dangle in front of Jesus' face: "To you I will give all this authority and their glory, for it has been delivered to me, and I give it to whom I will".[28] Here the enemy makes the big mistake of offering the world to the one who already rightly owns it—that is, to the Son of God. At the end of Jesus' ministry, when he had completed his work, Jesus would declare that all authority in heaven and earth had been given to him.[29] But here at the beginning, the devil, like some scheming boy stealing apples and trying to sell them back to their rightful owner, promises the Son of God the kingdoms of the world. The Tester gives Jesus the test: to gain his inheritance, he has to worship not God but the devil.

Every liar knows that the best lie is about 90% true. When the Evil One says the kingdoms of the world have been handed over to him to give to whomever he wants to give them (now, that's a mouthful!), Jesus does not respond by saying, "That's not true! Liar, liar, pants on fire!" His answer appears to accept the truth of what the devil says, but to reject the course of action suggested by him as a consequence. Jesus himself later called Satan "the ruler of this world",[30] and Paul would even call him "the god of this world".[31]

Now, neither Jesus nor Paul would deny that God, the Father of Jesus Christ, was truly in charge of this world. There is no 'dualism' in the Bible, with God and the devil being equal and opposite forces arrayed against each other, as suggested by the (rather exciting!) Christian novels of Frank Perretti. God never loses control. This is always his world. But it is a fallen world and God has answered our sin with his judgement. And part of this judgement is to deliver the world over to Satan. We will be talking more about how this works before too long. But for now, it is like the situation illustrated in the book of Job, where God grants Satan permission to harm Job, and take away his family and health, while at the same time maintaining his supreme rule of the world and his care for Job. God is always in ultimate control and human beings are always firmly under his loving care, but he has permitted the devil an enormous influence. In a real sense, the world has been given (that is, by God) to the devil. He is the one who has led the whole world astray, and so the whole world is under his control.[32] He is the prince of this world, and we have all fallen into his slavery.

Now, the mechanism by which the devil gains this control over us, or by which we give him this control, will be explained further in the next chapter; but for the present we need to notice the terrible facts that are placed before us here: the world given to the devil; the whole world led astray; the whole world under the devil's control.

If this is true, then perhaps we might expect to see lots of satanic manifestations breaking out everywhere all over the world: evil, monstrous creatures with foul breath and wings, flashes of fire, spooky incarnations and possessions. We might expect our world to resemble the set of one of those 'satanic slash horror' films.

But this is not how Satan works. The normal way he works, is, well, normally! And, I should also say, attractively! There is nothing terribly compelling about an ugly, smelly, fire-breathing monstrosity (except, perhaps, to another ugly, smelly, fire-breathing monstrosity, or to its mum). But one of the great deceptions of the Great Deceiver is that he disguises himself as "an angel of light".[33] Have you noticed that he is all about appearances? (And have you noticed that our world is increasingly obsessed with style over substance, form rather than content, looking good rather than being good. Interesting.) Satan wants to look good: his 'angel of light' garb is the Armani suit of the underworld. He also wants us to look good, promising all the kingdoms of this world *and their glory*— that is, their attractive appearance, the things that draw us to these kingdoms. If Tony Soprano, boss of the criminal underworld, is clever enough to exploit people's weaknesses by giving them exactly what they want, which then results in their own slavery and destruction, then how much more the prince of the underworld?

In other words, instead of fearing satanic *possession*, we should be deeply worried about *being normal*. This is the real concern. We become slaves and servants of the devil just by being normal human beings, and doing what normal human beings do. Adopting strategies that have been perfected over the centuries, he has been working at securing our slavery since the moment we were born. No, longer than that—since the moment our ancestors were born.

Feel the tragedy in that famous encounter between the apostle Peter and the Lord Jesus on the road near Caesarea Philippi.[34] The incident begins with Jesus conducting an opinion poll, "Who do people say that I am?" The disciples enjoy being able to tell him what they had been hearing from the crowds. Then a different, more pointed question: "But who do you say that I am?"

True to form, Peter answers straight away, "You are the Christ". If the John 3:16 guy had been in the crowd, he would have been proud of that answer! Jesus was God's long-awaited king, who would bring the salvation that humanity so badly needed. Jesus affirms Peter: this was exactly who he was, and at last one of his disciples had seen the light. This was good news.

But then Jesus begins to reveal that his future is not going to be all that bright: betrayal, torture, mockery, and being killed by the authorities of the land. This is too much for Peter, who takes his master aside and rebukes him. At that point, Jesus gives Peter a counter-rebuke—and this is where it gets really interesting for our purposes of understanding the underworld and its master. Jesus turns to Peter and says, "Get behind me, Satan! For you are not setting your mind on the things of God, but on the things of man." Or, to put it another way, 'You aren't thinking like God; you are thinking like a human being'.

Now, if you think about it, this sounds like Jesus is being pretty rough on Peter. He calls him 'Satan'. Why?

Because he is thinking like a human being? Well, how can he be blamed for that? Isn't that exactly what he is?

I once had a pest control man who told me that you only get rid of cockroaches by thinking like a cockroach. It was the first time I had met someone who was proud of being able to do that. I guess that counts as a pretty extreme cross-cultural experience (if cockroaches have 'culture'). It is exactly the opposite here. Peter is not being accused of being cross-cultural. Here Peter is accused of being thoroughly and completely cultural. He is thinking just like a human being, and that is exactly what he is! But here Jesus exposes the terrible situation that we are in. To think in a typically human way is to be on the side of Satan rather than God.

Peter is simply thinking as he has been trained to think. He sees the world as he has always seen it. He thinks from within that framework. He thinks according to his family upbringing, his education, his common sense, his proverbial wisdom, the common human experience he has gained from life. He uses all the experience and resources that would have usually made him get ahead in the world to rebuke Jesus for being so pessimistic about the fate of the Christ. And for his trouble, Peter just gets an ear-bashing. Where's the respect?

Peter is thinking like a human being. The whole world lies in the power of the evil one. All the kingdoms and all their glory are his. By the time we come to any moment of decision, we are already ensnared in the devil's ways, because the world that we call home is so deeply enthralled that to think like a human being is to think exactly how the devil wants us to think. We are held captive by him to do his will.

And, of course, this captivity to the prince of the underworld is only made possible by our own underworld. Remember the beast that lies within. This is the human heart. We don't need any dramatic possession by an outside underworld being. The desires and attitudes and motivations of the heart are already sold down the river. The whole world is under the devil's charge and what we might see as 'natural' is used in his service. Just to be human is to be enslaved to the devil.

The New Testament brings the underworld into our own world, and merges them together. Secular life is riddled with the underworld, because all the kingdoms of the earth have been given over to the devil. It makes our situation even worse. And when modern Western men or women refuse to acknowledge a spiritual realm as they blindly champion the cause of a secular society, the devil is laughing on both sides of his maw. This is one of his basic lies: "The fool says in his heart, 'There is no God'".[35] Another is like it: "let us make a name for ourselves".[36] We seek to build secular society by our own ingenuity and power alone, but whether we like it or not, or know it or not, we are on the payroll of the master of the underworld.

One of the most amusing things about *The Sopranos* is the strange, twisted logic that operates in this criminal underworld. At face value, it sounds perfectly coherent, and has its own sense of order and process. Take, for example, the tried and true practice known as 'protection'. If the pizza parlour owner keeps paying his regular weekly contribution, then his business won't suffer any untimely accidents, nor will he. It is simple, clearly communicated, and relentlessly logical. But it is also out of step with the larger reality. When we move out of the 'logic' of the underworld into the 'logic' of the larger universe, then 'protection' becomes a strange twisted distortion of reality that is evil and destructive.

Or take the scene where young Chrissy is not seeing eye to eye with his Captain, Paulie. He is annoyed that Paulie lavishly entertains a big party in a restaurant and expects Chrissy to pay the bill because them's the rules. Chrissy pays, but argues about it once they are outside. When the waiter comes out to complain about the tiny tip he received, this is too much. The waiter ends up dead in the car park. Chrissy and Paulie go home, the event having brought them together again. Isn't that nice—conflict resolution at its finest! Two work colleagues able to bury their differences so they can get along for another day. But that was not the only thing that had to be buried.

There is an *absurdity* about evil. The devil is anti-word, anti-rationality.[37] But that doesn't mean that everything he does seems irrational when viewed in isolation. He is able to construct a world that seems logical, rational, and that has its own internal order and process. It has its power, its authority, and its appearance is glorious. It seems a "delight to the eyes", and is desirable "to make one wise"—and wealthy and powerful and important and secure.[38] It offers its own rewards. It is the world as we know it. And yet it is out of step with reality. For this is God's world, and a world operating without its Creator is as absurd as the *Sopranos'* system of 'protection'. This world operating without God is like resolving conflict by leaving a dead body in the car park.

We are under Satan's dominion because we are sinners. But it is absolutely useless to call upon us sinners to change our ways. We cannot. We have fallen into the devil's hands, we are held captive to do his will, and we willingly and naturally want to do it, because this is what it is to be a human being. Normal life is part of our slavery and brings us more slavery. We are so captivated that we don't even know that we are enslaved. We actually believe that his ways are 'normal', the best ways. Here is the real tragedy of human life. We have fallen, fallen into an irretrievable state. Our sinful heart has led to our downfall. Our *hamartia* has delivered us over to the 'protection' of the underworld, and the 'protection' of the prince of demons. We are under 'protection' from the one who is a liar and a murderer from the beginning. He deceives in order to kill.

How did we get to this situation? How does the devil use ordinary means to trap us into his service, to get us to do his will? What is his key? It all has to do with him wielding the power of death, and using our fear of death to bring us further and further into his slavery. That will be the subject of our next chapter.

But before we leave the master of the underworld, it is worthwhile turning again from the margins to the middle.

Once in Israel's history, a gigantic warrior named Goliath stepped onto the battlefield.[39] He was huge, with biceps the size of thighs. He taunted the armies of Israel, who were speechless from fear at the size of this man. He would act as the champion of the Philistine army, and he yelled for Israel's champion to fight against him! Whoever won the one-on-one would win the war.

The opening scene of the movie *Troy* (2004) depicts a similar scene, with pretty-boy Brad Pitt as an unlikely Achilles, slaying the champion on the opposite side. Later, the Greek Achilles would also slay the Trojan Hector. One champion against another, with implications for the people they represent.

And as Jesus taught about his coming death, he used the same kind of language of champions. He had come 'to plunder the strong man's house',[40] and in his death the "ruler of this world" would be cast out.[41] In the strangest battle in all of history, fought on the strangest of battlefields, the champion of the underworld was defeated by a crucified man, dying in the air, with his arms stretched out to all of humanity.

CHAPTER 5

The Underworld of Death

*Y*OU CANNOT TALK about the criminal underworld without talking about death. When you boil it all down to the basics, the 'respect' that Tony Soprano commands and demands does not come from his charming personality or his good family upbringing. Neither does it come from his ability to bash the biggest guy in the clubhouse as part of his post-operative physio regimen.

Everybody knows that Mr Biceps—younger, fitter, stronger, angrier—could have beaten the tar out of Tony—older, fatter, post-coma weaker, angrier (yes, it is hard to decide on that one). But he didn't. Why not? Because, quite simply, that would be a short-term life plan. That would be the kind of action that is probably gonna get ya whacked, iced, hit, disappeared, floating in the river, sleeping with the fishes, wearing cement shoes, 86'd, riding in the car boot, dealt with—you get the idea.

First-century philosopher Epictetus once observed about the Italian in charge in his day: "No-one fears Caesar himself, but they fear death, banishment, loss of goods, prison, disgrace".[42] The present-day New Jersey Italians would echo his sentiments: the boss rules by fear, and the fear by which he rules is ultimately the fear of death.

Death, of course, has a way of sneaking up on you. The one who holds the power of your death also begins to hold the power of your life. If a debt is not paid, pain can be administered, legs can be broken, digits can be removed. If a point needs to be made, more pain can be delivered, arms can be broken, family members can be threatened. If someone wants to get out of 'the family', plenty more pain is set aside for this eventuality—ribs can be fractured, businesses firebombed. The beauty of holding the power of death is that it doesn't have to be administered all at once; there is plenty of time to gradually parcel it out. After all, if you can keep a punk alive, there is more chance of 'persuading' him to become a 'nice little earner'.

In the classic underworld, death is also the main issue of concern. This is the real point of all the features of the underworld. To go to the underworld is to die. To think about underworld beings is to think about who—or what—you might meet in the world of the dead. To think about the master of the underworld is to think about the one who has been mixed up with death from the beginning.

And, once again, underworld death has a way of sneaking up on you. It doesn't come all at once. There are plenty of ways for its pains to be delivered early. The underworld beings can invade the life of the living, inflicting their ghostly pain for whatever evil purposes they—or someone else—may have in mind. And behind it all, somehow, is the master of the underworld, the devil, who deceives the living in order to destroy them. And he is just as smart as Tony: no point doing it all at once. If you can keep a punk alive, then there is more chance of him becoming a nice little earner.

Death is the main issue. The one who holds the power of death uses the fear of death to bring others into a lifetime of slavery. Ultimately, it is death that we need to understand, and if the Christian message is worth believing it must say something worth hearing about our last and greatest enemy.

I remember standing at the graveside of an elderly relative. He had been a lifetime member of a men's 'club' (for want of a better word). At a certain point in the graveside ceremony, the Christian minister stepped back and a representative of the club stepped forward to say a few words. He said something like this: "If there is anything after the grave, we hope our brother is part of it". After a lifetime of gathering together, talking about the philosophy promoted by the 'club', and doing good together, this is the best they can say? "*If* there is ...we *hope* ...?" For some reason, at that moment I learnt a lesson that has never left me. If your philosophy of life has nothing to say at the graveside, then it has nothing to say. Here is our last and greatest enemy. The grave casts a shadow over our life and questions its whole existence. This is the problem that has invaded our world. Is there any hope? Is there any help? Is there a way to 'descend' into the underworld, and to come out of it still alive?

We have been dabbling around in the dark underworld that keeps intruding at the outskirts of the New Testament. We would probably like to know more about the underworld spaces, poking through out there on the periphery, but we are not given much information. Perhaps we are confused about the various underworld beings touched on at the margins of the New Testament, but although a little bit more is said about the beings than the spaces, we still don't have enough to answer all our questions. Still more is said about the master of the underworld, and this dark figure brings us closer to the centre of the New Testament message—but not because we are given a clear, front-on look at him. We are closer because Satan is the one the Son of God came to destroy.

When we turn to death, however, we have arrived at the major category by which the underworld is to be understood. This is the point of all the associated imagery, metaphors and descriptions of the classic underworld. Even though we may not learn everything about death, here we step even closer to the centre of the New Testament message. For God so loved the world, that he gave his only Son, so that anyone who believes in him *should not perish but have eternal life.* Here is a message that speaks so loudly at the graveside that it even has the power to waken the dead.

ONE OF THE STRANGE THINGS ABOUT DEATH IS THAT although it is a universal feature of human life, it is difficult to say exactly what it is. It is the end of life, but is that when we breathe our last breath? Or is it when the heart stops, or the brain ceases its activity? And philosophically, or even theologically, what is death?

What was once a person, with all the value and significance that comes from being a person, created in God's image, is now 'gone'. But—the old question emerges again—where have they gone, and how is this possible? Is death like a long sleep, or is it more like a coma? Or is it simply annihilation, with the grave being our eternal home, an eternal home full of worms, rottenness, decay and the filthy uncleanness of the underworld? Is it the separation of the spirit from the body—the soul returning to the air and then to the upper atmosphere, dwelling as far 'aloft' as is possible, according to the extent of its purity? Was the ancient saying right when it said that the body goes downwards while the soul flies upwards?

There are traces of all of these aspects of death in the Bible. Once again, the ancient views poke through at the margins, but we don't gain any really clear definition of death amongst those marginal smatterings. Perhaps this is because rather than describing *what* death is, the Bible is more interested in explaining *why* it is.

One thing it does say clearly, however, is that death is not just a 'natural part of life'. This was the ancient Stoic philosophy, and it has become the most prevalent view in Western society through the enormous influence of Elisabeth Kübler-Ross and others. One thing the Stoics had going for them was that they were realistic. They understood that the world was not a happy place; that it was filled with pain. They knew that ultimately our pain was caused by the grave. In the first century, the average life expectancy at birth was about 20-25 years, such were the ravages of disease. The Stoics were well aware that they were living on borrowed time, constantly under the shadow of the grave. You take a wife, but someone is likely to take her from you, perhaps for a fleeting moment's pleasure to release him from his pain; or perhaps so that he—or she—can prove to themselves they are still young. Your wife becomes pregnant, and she might die in childbirth, along with her child. She survives childbirth, but the baby doesn't— and this cycle could be repeated in the one family, over and over again. If your baby boy is born safely, he only has a 30-40% chance of reaching his first birthday. If he survives until one, unlike half of his kindergarten class, he might survive until he is ten. If he survives until he is ten, then he must be pretty strong—only about 40% of those born reached 20-25. And then along comes tuberculosis and kills him in his twenties.

The ravages of death taught the ancient world about loss. The Stoic was realistic about this. His philosophy prized *autarky*, 'sufficiency in oneself, independence' (which is not to be confused with *autarchy*, 'self rule'). Since the contemporary Western world has drunk so deeply of Stoicism (without perhaps always being conscious of doing so), this quality just sounds normal to us—and from our last chapter, that in itself ought to ring a warning bell! We prize self-sufficiency and independence as a quality of freedom.

The Stoic also prized *autarky* as freedom, but for slightly different reasons. In a shifting, changing, suffering world, what was 'yours' could suddenly be taken away. In this world under the shadow of death, if you got too attached to anything, where would you be when you (almost inevitably) lost it? The Stoic Epictetus was clear: if you didn't manage to be detached from the things and people around you, then they had power over you, and so you weren't truly free. To gain *autarky*, it was the Stoic's daily duty to practise *detachment and distancing* from everyone and everything around him:

> This should be our study from morning to night, beginning from the least to the frailest things, from an earthen vessel, from a glass. Afterwards proceed to a suit of clothes, a dog, a horse, an estate; from thence to your self, body, parts of the body, children, wife, brothers. Look everywhere around you, and throw them from yourself. Correct your principles. See that nothing cleave to you which is not your own; nothing grow to you that may give you pain when it is torn away. And say, when you are daily exercising yourself as you do here, not that you act the philosopher (admit this to be an insolent title), but that you are asserting your freedom.
> (*The Discourses*, IV.i.13)

In the name of freedom, detach yourselves from anything or anyone "that may give you pain when it is torn away". The Roman emperor Marcus Aurelius, another Stoic, was particularly grabbed by another saying of Epictetus—although he didn't say it in the movie *Gladiator* (2000), I noticed. It brings out the tragic realism of these guys, trying to cope with a world ruled by death:

> When you kiss your child goodnight, say, "He could be dead in the morning".

Marcus Aurelius was no armchair philosopher on this point. He was a father who suffered the loss of four children in their infancy. Standing at the bedside must have brought back deep wells of pain for him. And so even at a moment that should have been filled with intimacy—saying goodnight to your child—it was better to practise detachment.

The Stoic philosophy of *autarky* gives us a very clear example of how the fear of death can corrupt life itself. These guys were copers, pain-minimizers. Although they did have a strong morality, which included a clear sense of doing the right thing by others, and which valued friendship highly, could relationships really flourish with someone deliberately practising *detachment*? Relationships are built with *engagement*, *involvement*, and *sympathy*—that fellow-feeling that is prepared to risk the potential pain, and is willing to absorb that pain out of a genuine love of the other. Yes, all of this must come out of a healthy sense of self and not out of our own 'dependency issues', but this is far from the *autarky* that insisted on daily detachment exercises. The fear of death, the avoidance of pain, distancing and detachment: this is not freedom. This is far from life and life to the full.

For the Stoic, the death of a child was as natural as the corn harvest. Why should it provoke any more grief than that? The task of life was to seek after *autarky*, even when faced with such a family disaster; to so suppress the emotions that a response to your dead child was the same as a response to bringing in the corn. Just part of life. Just the end of life. A natural part of life.

This same approach, albeit with a distinctively 20th-century twist, has been widely propagated by the teaching and writing of Elisabeth Kübler-Ross and her school. The task of the helping professions is to assist the dying patient to move towards acceptance of this final stage of the 'natural' life-cycle. Sure, there are various stages that they will go through; there will be an immature resistance to death being natural, but with time and care we can help them move towards seeing their own death, or the death of their loved ones, as being as natural as the corn harvest.

How different this approach is from that of our poets. "Do not go gently into that dark night; Rage, Rage, Rage against the dying of the light!" wrote Dylan Thomas. And somehow that captures what we all instinctively feel in the presence of death. How different, too, is the attitude of Jesus himself, who stood at the graveside of his friend Lazarus, and not only wept but was angry[43]—angry at the damage, the disruption, the destruction caused by death let loose amongst human beings. For death is far from natural. According to the apocalyptic unveiling of reality that helps us to see the world from God's point of view, death is a disruption. It was never meant to be. It is right for us to feel it deeply, to mourn when it takes others away from us, to rage, rage, rage against its presence in this world. It is right to long for it to be gone, so that the world can be different, and we can truly live. Death brings us loss, and living in the shadow of the grave, we are lost.

The New Testament proclaims its message of God's love against the black backdrop of a world afflicted by the horrors of an unnatural death. Jesus announced motto-like that he had come "to seek and save the lost".[44] And we have already come across that famous sports-lover verse more than once: "For God so loved the world that he gave his only Son, that whoever believes in him should not perish but have eternal life".[45] The central message of the New Testament speaks directly to this blemish in the midst of human life—this corruption that cuts a path through our families, and fills our bedsheets with tears. It tells us that God has found a way to stop us from perishing. Death is so unnatural that God has done something to rid his world of it.

Even if it doesn't give us answers to all the philosophical questions we might have about death, the New Testament gives us clear answers to the practical problem of the death we all face. It informs us about death at the same instant that it tells us about God's solution: "the wages of sin is death, but the free gift of God is eternal life in Christ Jesus our Lord".[46]

This is a key statement. It helps us to understand this blight with which we are afflicted. If death is unnatural, why do we die? Here is the answer. Death is the wages of sin. Death is the consequence of our sin. And this consequence, according to the biblical take on reality, must be regarded as the punishment of God upon this world for rejecting its creator—*our* creator.

One of the foundational stories in the Bible is the account of Adam and Eve in the garden of Eden (in Genesis 2 and 3). After God created the world, he gave Adam a special place in it, to rule the world on his behalf, in company with Eve. The narrative shows God graciously warning Adam that there was one tree in the garden that was not healthy for him to eat: "of the tree of the knowledge of good and evil you shall not eat, for in the day that you eat of it you shall surely die".[47] As the famous story goes on to show, Adam and Eve fell for the deception that God's word was not good for them, and in an act of self-determination and out of a desire to break free from God, they ate of this fruit. And the rest, as they say, is our sad history.

Many years later, the apostle Paul summed up the significance of this event: "sin came into the world through one man, and death through sin".[48] The story of Adam's 'fall' is not just about his disobedience to God's command; it is about the introduction of the *hamartia*, the fatal flaw, that has afflicted each and every one of us ever since. The pattern in the garden of Eden is the same for all of us today: we question God's word, we wonder whether his ways are really the best thing for us (according to our standards of 'normality'), and we then decide to go our way rather than God's way. And so the world's problems continue.

Quite frequently Christians have explained the consequences of Adam's fall by the introduction of a category that is, in the end, quite unhelpful. God warned Adam that on the day he ate of the fruit, he would surely die. But when Adam and Eve ate the fruit— so the argument goes—they didn't drop dead on the spot, but lived on for quite some time. Instead, they were simply cast out of the garden, 'separated' from God's presence (funny how the language of 'space' crops up everywhere). In other words, it is said, they experienced 'spiritual death' not physical death.

But this is not what is going on here at all. Not only does this explanation introduce a mysterious concept called 'spiritual death' that requires an equally mysterious explanation; more seriously, it underestimates the significance of 'physical death'. These kinds of explanations tend to speak as if the Stoics and Elisabeth Kübler-Ross and her team were right—*physical* death is a natural part of life; it is just the *spiritual* death (whatever that may be) that is the problem!

When Paul spoke of sin coming into the world, "and death through sin", it was not 'spiritual death' he was talking about but death *full stop*. The fact that our Adam and Eve did not drop dead on the spot is a rather irrelevant observation, for immediately after their sin, they were subjected to a world in which death reigns. The judgements of God pronounced in Genesis 3 all speak of the painful, dying world which had now become reality for them and their descendants: painful work for Adam, painful childbirth for Eve, painful marriage for both of them. The ground is now cursed because of them, and their destiny is to return to the ground, to die. Dust to dust. The world has become a terrifying place to live in, with the ever-present threat of violence and death at the hands of others—even those you love. And, when we come to Adam's genealogy,[49] no matter how long any one of his descendants might have lived, or how many children they may have begotten (or is it begatted?), the chorus reveals the true state of the continual reality of human existence: "and he died … and he died … and he died".[50] Sin entered the world, and death through sin.

The problem of death is not simply that we will die one day. That would reduce our problem to a moment, an event, rather than a state of existence. The problem is that we carry the grave within us. For we are mortal, and our mortality rots away our existence from the moment we are born. As the funeral service puts it: "in the midst of life, we are in death".

Death threatens us externally. The daily news brings before us the same old stories, with only the names and places changed to vary the regular diet of violence, disorder and death. We are constantly reminded of our precarious, knife-edge existence. Although some manage to escape taxes, death is the one true constant in human society. It will eventually take everyone. It is indiscriminate, and when it comes, it seems that we always die 'suddenly and unprepared'. The "king of terrors", as it is described in Job,[51] takes the old and the young, males and females, the unhealthy and the healthy, all races and ages, all religions and cultures. When it is time to go, it is time to go. And death waits for no-one.

But death does not stay 'out there' in the world. It slinks closer to our own circle. A family member dies; a parent contracts cancer; a sister has a miscarriage; a brother a road accident; a cousin a long-term disability; a friend a sporting mishap. Now it is not just a threat out there, but it is something we feel personally. We know the loss, we grieve over it, it affects us deep down. Once we are touched by it, we are changed.

But the presence of death is even more pervasive. It is there in our bodily ailments and illnesses, which are a constant reminder of our mortality. It is there in our questions about meaning and purpose, for, if we stop to think about it, the grave seems to undermine everything we might achieve. So it questions our whole existence.

Death is there in the relational debris that seems to fall out on the road behind us as we move through life. Again, our poets have pointed this out:

> The sky is torn across
> This ragged anniversary of two
> Who moved for three years in tune
> Down the long walks of their vows.

Now their love lies a loss
And Love and his patients roar on a chain;
From every true or crater
Carrying cloud, Death strikes their house.
(Dylan Thomas, 'On a Wedding Anniversary')

Thomas is saying that death is more than just a metaphor for a relationship coming to an end. People mourn relational breakdown just as surely as they mourn death itself. Sometimes—no, quite often—relationships are destroyed by moral failings, affairs, brutality, emotional cruelty, and the like; sometimes not. But whatever the surface cause, it is the sign of the deeper problem that afflicts us.

I remember hearing an interview with Spike Milligan, Australian comedian and member of the long-running *Goon Show*, which changed the face of British comedy. He spoke sadly about his long-term suffering under the oppression of mental illness. He looked back on a time when he was aware of his marriage failing: "I knew I was doing something that was killing my marriage, but I couldn't work out what it was". *Killing* my marriage. Death can invade our relationships, bringing structural problems that no moralistic exhortation, or talk-therapy, or medication, or good-will can ever possibly fix. The relational breakdown is yet another way the grave takes our life away far too early.

But death pushes further than our relational circle. Despite our fears of being 'possessed' by an external force, death is a presence within our very body from the moment we take our first breath. How many babies are born with severe difficulties already built into their tiny frames? Despite the medical advances since Jesus' day, children still get sick and die. We all suffer from illness, and are susceptible to viral and bacterial attack. We have our bodily weaknesses, our emotional weaknesses, and like poor Spike Milligan we have our mental weaknesses too.

Yes, I know, we are all supposed to be politically correct about these things. We are not to talk in a way that excludes others because of some 'different' quality of life they have been dealt. So, for example, rather than being derogatory about a moustache-less man's masculinity, I have learned to say that most other men are 'moustache challenged'. It is, however, one thing to say that a person is of no lesser value because of their 'challenges'; it is quite another to say that those 'challenges' are good in themselves. What blind person wouldn't like to see the delights and colour of a flower, having smelled its scent? What deaf person wouldn't like to hear the sound of their lover's voice, having watched their lips so closely? What lame person wouldn't want to walk, or run, or even slam-dunk a basketball? The various 'challenges' are still 'challenges', and for these equally valued human beings they do diminish the possibilities of life to the full.

We are mortal. And because we are mortal, we live under the shadow of death every single day of our lives. And this is where we open ourselves up for further disaster.

As we have already seen, Jesus the friend of sinners pointed to the problem of the human heart. Inside us all we have the rottenness of *hamartia*, the fatal flaw that will be the death of us one day, and is the death of us every day. In a strange twist, death also increases the flaw. Because we are mortal, there is a profound instability at the core of our being, a profound insecurity.

Just think for a minute about someone who has to live under some kind of uncertainty. Say they hear a rumour that the company is about to 'downsize' and they fear their long lunch breaks, late starts and early home-times might count against them ever so slightly. You can imagine, in every single one of their 1000 personal phone calls made each day on the boss's time, what subject their conversation will turn to. Or the uncertainty that arises over complications in childbirth, or when a marriage looks like it is over, or when there is the threat of war, or the prospect of a relative being caught in a foreign city in a terrorist bombing. What happens when the world as we know it changes in such a defining and foundational way? Uncertainty destabilizes life. We don't like instability and we try to resolve it.

We are mortal, or 'flesh', as the New Testament calls us. And with the grave as our only prospect, as people with no future, we are left with a profound uncertainty at our core, deep within our already problematic heart.

At one point the glorious centre of the New Testament is summarized as follows. It says:

> Since therefore the children share in flesh and
> blood, he himself likewise partook of the same
> things, that through death he might destroy the one
> who has the power of death, that is, the devil, and
> deliver all those who through fear of death were
> subject to lifelong slavery. (Heb 2:14-15)

This summary of the good news of Jesus Christ is exactly the kind of summary we need to hear as we think about living with the underworld. Here, at last, we can see how the Evil One, the murderer from the beginning, works to produce our slavery in the midst of 'ordinary life'. Notice how our problem is described: slavery to the master of the underworld, brought about by a profound internal distress, the fear of death.

How does this work? How does our fear of death bring us into slavery to the devil? This takes some thinking about.

Some will object, for example, that the 'fear of death' is not really such a huge problem. What if you aren't someone who is really afraid? Like the comedian Woody Allen, who once said: "I am not afraid of dying. I just don't want to be there when it happens."

Most people who seem unaffected by the fear of death manage to keep up their brave face by not thinking about it. Like a friend of mine who once told me she doesn't think about the possibility of her death at all: "If I did that, I would go crazy". Doesn't her answer, in fact, show that at least occasionally she *has* thought about it? At some point, she tiptoed up to the abyss and was unhinged by the horror of what she saw there. Her complete lack of answers in the face of death made her shrink back from further contemplation.

But what about those who seem to have no fear at all, no fear of anything! I knew someone once who even went with his wife to the post-Christmas sales, for goodness sake! Psychologists tell us, of course, that the rest of us need to be afraid of someone who is not afraid—we might have a sociopath on our hands. They are not afraid because the distortion within them has turned them into an extreme case.

Other slightly less extreme cases cope with the

prospect of death by staring it in the face and daring it to take them—like people who throw themselves out of planes under a flimsy canopy of silk, or off a bridge with an elastic band on their ankle. We still call these 'extreme sports', and they excite some people precisely because of the fear of death. Like my friend, they tiptoe up to the edge of the abyss, but rather than shrinking back they stay just close enough to get a rush of adrenalin from the fear.

But why go to such extreme examples? What about Mr Joe and Mrs Jo Average, just struggling to make a living in some ordinary suburb? We say we are a *materialistic* society, a society of rampant *consumers*. But that is just our surface problem. If we scratch below the surface, with the aid of our apocalyptic unveiling, what do we find? Let the friend of sinners speak for himself:

> Therefore do not be anxious, saying, 'What shall we eat?' or 'What shall we drink?' or 'What shall we wear?' For the Gentiles seek after all these things, and your heavenly Father knows that you need them all. But seek first the kingdom of God and his righteousness, and all these things will be added to you.
>
> Therefore do not be anxious about tomorrow, for tomorrow will be anxious for itself. Sufficient for the day is its own trouble. (Matt 6:31-34)

Jesus ties the desperate quest for the staples of consumerism (food, drink, clothing) to an underlying anxiety. It is an anxiety about tomorrow, about survival. This is the fear of death in another form. For otherwise, why would the kingdom of God, the new creation, be the alternative?

What about the person who is the 'life of the party'— any fear here? The party animals not only brave the post-

Christmas sales; they laugh at them. And they snap up the best clothes, because they are an essential element in enjoying life to the full in the year ahead of them. They want to suck the marrow out of life, to minimize the pain by maximizing the pleasure. They are the person who says—in the words of the old slogan thrown at the Epicureans—"Come, let us eat, drink and be merry". Fun, pleasure, laughter, good times, good food, good wine, sexual experiences, bodily comforts, sunshine, gyms, gym-shaped bodies, gym clothes (or is that going too far?)—whatever it takes to 'maximize the pleasure'. But, hang on, what was the end of that old slogan? What is this mad pursuit of pleasure motivated by? "Come, let us eat, drink, and be merry *for tomorrow we die*."

The controversial heavy weight boxer, Mike Tyson, was once asked if he was afraid. "Everyone's afraid", he answered. "Both the coward and the brave man are afraid. It is not whether or not you are afraid that matters, it is what you do with it. The coward feels his fear and he runs. The brave man feels his fear, and he uses it against his opponent."

The same is true of the fear of death. Everyone is afraid—they just do different things with it. Some run from death by simply not thinking about it; some lie awake at night worrying about it; some stave it off with all kinds of busy activities; some try to cheat death by maximizing their pleasure before death comes; some turn and face death and dare it to take them. But everyone is afraid. Scratch down to the mortal flesh and you will find that deep anxiety, that fear of the grave that unsettles us to our very core.

This is the fear, says our writer to the Hebrews, that

leads to lifelong slavery. We are afraid, and we long for some kind of security, some safe place to stand. We are wide open to anyone or anything that can offer us this security, who can promise us something that might ward off the threat of the grave. At this point, we begin to see the power the devil wields. The master of the underworld has us eating out of his hand. He is the one who deceives in order to kill. He can make plenty of deceptive promises that cater for our desire for security.

Jesus was well aware of these false promises of security, and he was constantly talking against them. The false security brought about by wealth, or position, or family connection, or political power, or education, or possessions, or status in the eyes of others. There are the slightly less reputable ones, such as personal egotistical power, conquest, and the thrill of destroying others, but let's leave these ones aside. For there are also plenty of more fashionable ones, such as land and property, home extensions, job security, sexual pleasure, spending power, the secure love of a family—and we could go on. It's all the structures of what we call 'ordinary life', all the things we are brought up to believe in, to trust in; all the normal everyday options presented to us by "the kingdoms of the world and their glory". [52]

Now it all comes together! Because of our sin, the world lies under the sentence of death, a sentence we carry around with us in our mortal flesh. This causes a profound disruptive anxiety, a fear of death, that may be expressed in different ways, and masked in different ways, but is always there. This fear of death makes us long for security, for something that will calm our fears. We are security-seeking missiles, and this opens us up to believe the lies of the devil, who tells us that our security is to be found in the things of this world. And, of course, these are all his to give, because this world belongs to him. At that point, our fear of death has taken us to exactly where the master of the underworld wants us: we are his slaves.

This is our tragic situation, from which we can never escape. We fear death and its inevitability. We know that the psalmist was right when he described the grave as having an appetite, never satisfied, with jaws that close in on us.[53] It waits to take all of us, and no-one can escape. No ransom can be paid to avoid it.[54] The underworld eats away at our existence, and so we end up enslaved to the master of the underworld, held captive to do his will.

'To do his will'—that is, his anti-God will. For our slavery then takes another turn. Our slavery to the devil is itself the root of all kinds of sin. Not only do we die because we sin, but we also sin because we die. To put it another way—and with careful attention to our spelling—our *mortality* leads to *immorality*. Think of the Epicureans, whose fear of death leads to pleasure-seeking. How many other people are used and abused to serve their pleasure? Think of the daredevil, who challenges death to take him. How many others are put at risk, how many relationships and responsibilities and duties are forgotten by this reckless endangerment? Think of the materialistic consumer, whose desire for survival leads to the greedy cycle of ensuring one's own survival at the cost of the survival of so many others.

The apostle Paul pointed out that when we let *hamartia* loose 'in our mortal bodies', the result is that *we obey the desires of those mortal bodies*.[55] And, without any future other than the rottenness and filth of the grave, the desires of the mortal body are quite simple: survival, staving off the underworld. Our fundamental anxiety about the grave produces this fundamental desire to survive, expressed in all kinds of subsidiary desires: what can I eat, what can I wear, where can I live, how can I feel better about myself, how can I drown out the ticking of the clock that signals the inevitability of the grave? And as we pursue these desires, we don't mind using and abusing people in order to get them.

And so our *mortality* works *immorality*, bringing further evil consequences to our lives. The underworld ahead brings the underworld within, and through the very ordinary things of this world, we find ourselves enslaved to the underworld master. Deceived, in order to be killed. Dying, even while we live. In the midst of life, we are in death.

This is yet again why the moralists of this world can never help us. Moralists tend to focus only on issues of *immorality* (watch the spelling!). But lurking behind our *immorality* is our lack of *immortality* (watch it again). If you cannot deal with human *mortality*, then you will never produce human *morality*. If you cannot give us *immortality*, you will always have our *immorality*. And it will need to be something powerful that happens, because nobody can be scolded or exhorted or self-improved out of the grave. Death destroys the good life. The good life will only come if death can be destroyed.

On 3rd April, in the year AD 33, at about three o'clock in the afternoon, a man was hanging, up in the air, on a cross, with his hands outstretched to the world. As he died, he let out a blood-curdling cry that chilled the bystanders to their bones. "It is finished", he cried.[56]

And as we live our knife-edge existence, with death and the underworld all around us; as we long for a way of escape, we can only sigh and say, "Finished? I just wish that it was."

In order to help us to live, we need to find a way to live with the underworld. But that will require death to be defeated, and the master of the underworld to be neutralized. In other words, we don't just need renovation or moral improvement; we need resurrection. But where are we going to find that?

102 ↓ LIVING WITH THE UNDERWORLD

CHAPTER 6

Neutralizing the Underworld

*S*O MY DAUGHTER'S underworld and my own, the criminal and the classic, are more closely entwined than at first glance we thought—not simply because both have been the subject of movie interest for a long time, nor because at the present time they both seem to be fascinating our small and large screen viewers ('small' and 'large' being applied to the screens, not the viewers). There is a more profound connection between the two. The criminal underworld speaks of the evils that lie within humanity. *The Sopranos* shows us just how ordinary these criminals can be, and we ordinaries find ourselves entwined in their criminality. Perhaps Tony and his pals give vent to 'the beast within' in a more extreme form than all the Mr and Mrs Averages reading the mags in the waiting rooms of our health professionals. But we can all still recognize that the beast lurks within us all.

On the other hand, as we saw in Chapter 5, the

classic underworld points to the deep and underlying anxiety over death from which those evils ultimately spring. The beast within is in slavery to the beast below. To defeat the one, you need to defeat the other. But who can possibly perform that task? What hero might step forward to slay the beast?

"We don't need another hero", Tina Turner sang in *Mad Max: Beyond Thunderdome* (1985). I guess the world has seen too many already, without much visible success from any of them. Heroes have a habit of letting down their followers, and when heroes fall, their fall is usually of epic proportions and brings down many others in the process. Since the time of the Greek tragedies, we have been well aware of the fact that even heroes have their *hamartia*, their fatal flaw. No matter how strong, or brave, or handsome, or whatever other qualities they may excel in, they have their inner beast that will, eventually, bring them down like the rest of us. Tony Soprano knows this too: the criminal underworld would not be able to work like the well-oiled machine that it is if ordinary human beings didn't have vices that beg to be exploited.

Tina Turner wanted to know that there was "life beyond thunderdome". In the age of the nuclear bomb, the world grew darker under a foreboding sense of gloom. When such destructive technology was combined with humanity's 'beast within', would we eventually end up wiping ourselves totally off the face of the planet? Was there a possibility of life beyond the gloom of a world destined for the underworld?

The apocalyptic unveiling of reality from God's side tells us that this is exactly what we have with Jesus Christ. To know this, we need the apocalyptic unveiling. If we looked at Jesus without this unveiling, we may miss his significance completely. It has been called the scandal of Christianity that the God we Christians worship is someone who was an ordinary man; in fact, an ordinary man who suffered the indignity of being crucified. As it says in that famous passage from the Old Testament, Isaiah 53, we could look on this ordinary, crucified figure and say:

> ... he had no form or majesty that we should look
>   at him,
>   and no beauty that we should desire him.
> He was despised and rejected by men;
>   a man of sorrows, and acquainted with grief;
> and as one from whom men hide their faces
>   he was despised, and we esteemed him not.
> (Isa 53:2-3)

In his appearance, he was ordinary. In his suffering, he was repulsive. Nothing here to attract us to him. He lived like any other human being. He had a family, a home town, a trade, friends. He ate, he drank, he slept, he enjoyed a good celebration. He laughed, he cried, he got angry; he taught, he did good, and he ended up suffering unjustly at the hands of a man with absolute power, manipulated by other powerful men who were filled with jealousy. It is the tragic story of one of the many victims of our world. And when he died, it was horrendous. To be crucified was the worst way for anyone to die in the ancient world. Crucifixion aroused such horrible feelings that the word wasn't even mentioned in polite company. If we were there, we would have turned our faces away, like the people in Isaiah 53. But just being crucified wasn't really what made Jesus special. There were thousands of others at the time who suffered the same terrible fate.

And yet there was, without a doubt, something special about Jesus. Historians examine the evidence and try to explain why his name is still remembered and revered, when thousands of other people crucified in the first century have simply disappeared without trace. He certainly taught powerfully. He attracted great crowds—in fact, his ability to draw crowds was one of the things about him that was most disturbing to his enemies, and in the end, was a major factor in getting him killed. He also undoubtedly had the power to do some marvellous things: he certainly healed, he certainly had some power over the spirits. There were also stories of him performing amazing 'nature miracles' such as calming the storm. There were even a couple of reports that he had raised some people from the dead—one of them, Lazarus, was under threat of death (again!) because his resurfacing in the local cafés caused embarrassment to the authorities.

There were various theories around about the source of Jesus' teaching and power. His friends said one thing, his enemies another. This is important. Nobody disputed that he was saying and doing marvellous things. They simply disputed the source of his power. And so Jesus has left two very strong and diametrically opposed traces running through the historical sources: the New Testament and other writings associated with it say that he was the Son of God; other sources say that he must have been a sorcerer or magician. But notice carefully, both strands are not disputing the extraordinary things

Jesus did. They just have different explanations of their origin.

Despite the remarkable fuss that Jesus created during his lifetime, the major reason his name continues to be revered, and indeed why Christians continue to worship him as God, can be told quite simply. Three days after he died, his tomb was found empty, and he appeared to many people across a forty day period to prove that he had come back alive from the dead.

We really need to pause at this point and let this statement sink in. I have been hanging around church people for a long time now, and it seems that 'our kind' speaks of resurrection as if it is as natural as the corn harvest—or even more natural, because, come to think of it, I have never grown or harvested corn in my life.

Resurrection isn't natural. A long time ago now, I was a med student, attending an operation that started way too early in the morning, so early that the other med student didn't make the beginning of the procedure and missed the anaesthetic process ("There's an edge for me in the exams", I thought). Sometimes patients receive a general anaesthetic, but this time the guy was just knocked out from the waist down and somewhat sedated. My friend arrived and stood near the guy's head. The operation went on, and on, and after some time, the patient opened his eyes, turned to my friend and said, "Are they finished yet?" From the way my friend fell backwards in a dead faint, I guessed that he wasn't expecting this to happen.

So let's hear it again. Three days after Jesus died, his tomb was found empty, and he appeared to many people to prove that he had come back alive from the dead. If my friend didn't expect someone to wake up from an anaesthetic during an operation, how often do we expect someone to 'wake up' from the dead? The underworld doesn't have a revolving door. After centuries of human beings going into the underworld and never coming out again, this was truly remarkable—and even that must be the understatement of all time! But, for those of us who have lived a knife-edge existence with the underworld below and above and around us, and who have known for so long the tears of bereavement, this is exactly the event we have been longing for.

The apocalyptic unveiling of reality takes place around this event. If Jesus hadn't come back from the grave, then we would still be in the dark about the underworld, and, worse still, we would still be living in the darkness of the underworld. But Jesus' resurrection shines a piercing light into our death-filled gloom, and brings to human beings what the New Testament calls "a living hope".[57] And with that living hope comes an entirely new view of reality, as our eyes are opened, and the darkness of the underworld disappears. As the future begins to come into clearer focus, so the present begins to be transformed.

LET'S WIND BACK A LITTLE AND APPROACH THIS momentous event a little more slowly to understand it.

At its centre, the New Testament tells the good news of Jesus Christ bringing life to a dying world. There's that guy with the verse again in the grandstand: "For God so loved the world, that he gave his only Son, that whoever believes in him should not perish but have eternal life". With such a central message about 'not perishing', it is not really surprising that the gospel touches upon so many different aspects of the underworld: the underworld spaces, the underworld beings, the underworld master, and—the real focus of all this underworld stuff in the end—death itself. When the New Testament speaks of Jesus' ministry, it is like embarking on our tour of the underworld all over again, but this time it's as if we are taking the tour in the bus alongside Jesus himself, with him pointing out the highlights of his previous tour—and it was a tour of victory!

We don't need to spend much time explaining that Jesus lived a short and ordinary life in the first century of our era. He was born in Bethlehem, spent a little time in Egypt, grew up in Nazareth, moved to Capernaum and eventually died in Jerusalem.

But despite that real-world upbringing, when he spoke, he often used language that sounded like he had lived before. He spoke often of having "come" into the world with a purpose,[58] or to achieve a particular goal. Or, on the other side of this language, he spoke of God the Father having "sent" him into the world.[59] Later on, his apostles would speak of him "appearing" in this world.[60]

When the resurrection happened, the veil was pulled back and this language began to make more sense. Jesus was the Son of God, come into the world to bring about its salvation. Or, more dramatically, he was God who "became flesh and dwelt among us".[61] This is the other side of the scandal of Christianity: not just that we worship someone who was an ordinary man, but we worship that ordinary man because he was God.

Jesus' life and ministry is often described in the New Testament in the classic underworld language with which we are not so familiar. Jesus came down from above, from heaven, the realm of God the Father. Jesus spoke of returning back 'up' to this position, at the right hand of the Father. Before that could happen, he spoke of the necessity of his death. He died a crucified man and was buried as a corpse in a grave. The New Testament speaks of him descending to Hades, visiting the underworld, in the realms of the dead.[62] It even occasionally uses the term for the lowest spot of all, saying that he descended into the abyss.[63] And then, the resurrection began his 'journey' out of there, to ascend to the realms above from whence he had come. That is Jesus' 'underworld tour' in a nutshell.

But let's slow it down a little, so we can appreciate his journey just that little bit more. For centuries, Christians have remembered the incarnation (God became flesh) at Christmas time. This was the time that God 'came down' in order to save lost humanity. The writer to the Hebrews unveils a conversation between the Father and the Son before this moment, when the Son says, "a body have you prepared for me".[64] In order to enter into the human race, the eternal Son of God had to be given a body. That body was born, grew up and lived as Jesus of Nazareth.

And, of course, if he was truly going to identify with those he was about to save, it had to be a *mortal* body. In the words of Hebrews again, in the passage that is so important for understanding the underworld, we read: "Since therefore the children share in flesh and blood, he himself likewise partook of the same things".[65]

Existing like the rest of us, Jesus knew all the pains and tears of living as a mortal human being. He too was subject to the pressures of living under the shadow of the grave. He felt the testing, and he knew the temptation to find security in all the wrong places. He "learned obedience through what he suffered",[66] and he endured this suffering well. As a result, he is called "our great high priest", but he is not at all distant from us—"we do not have a high priest who is unable to sympathize with our weaknesses, but one who in every respect has been tempted as we are, yet without sin".[67] There is the key. Jesus found security in his Father's arms. He learned obedience, he was tested, and yet he was without sin. He lived the way all of us should have lived. Even though he was mortal, living with the constant pressure of the underworld, he lived the perfect human life.

The idea of God becoming mortal flesh is too much for us to understand. What could it have meant for the Son to enter the world and take on a mortal body? Paul tries to capture it in Philippians 2 by quoting what is possibly an early Christian hymn:

> ... Christ Jesus, who, though he was in the form of God, did not count equality with God a thing to be grasped, but made himself nothing, taking the form of a servant, being born in the likeness of men. And being found in human form, he humbled himself by becoming obedient to the point of death, even death on a cross. (Phil 2:5b-8)

Notice how the 'distance' he 'travelled' is stressed even further. The Son of God not only became a man, not only became a mortal man, not only died, but became "obedient to the point of death, even death on a cross".

This is what Christians have always remembered on Good Friday: Jesus died on the cross. Some early Christians, who lived and breathed the cosmology of their time, saw a significance in Jesus' crucifixion that perhaps nobody in our day would see. To be crucified was the only death in which you died in the air. Jesus dying in this way was symbolic, they said, of him 'cleansing the air' of all the spirits, ghosts and forces of evil that resided in that realm.[68] Now, instead of 'seeing' the air and fearing what it contained, the world could look up to the crucified Jesus, arms outstretched to the world, and realize that the air contained nothing to fear any more.

Everyone in the ancient world knew what crucifixion meant. Both Jew and Greek knew that a crucified person died under the curse of God. Why else would a person die so horribly? It must be because God's curse rested upon him! We should also recall that the crucified were considered to be good candidates for becoming ghosts, or restless spirits. They certainly couldn't expect a good position in the underworld. And this is where the Son of God descended to. Other parts of the New Testament have him going even further into the underworld, interacting with other underworld spirits who were perhaps awaiting punishment,[69] and descending even into the abyss itself, the lowest space of them all.[70]

In this massive 'descent', the Son of God goes from 'heaven' to 'hell', from the highest heavens to the deepest abyss—the full sweep of underworld possibilities. No-one else in the universe has 'fallen' this far. It's a journey unique to Jesus Christ. Whatever human sufferings are brought about by the underworld, Jesus has experienced them. When the Father prepared a body for him, it was a mortal body. Jesus lived as a human being, well aware of all the 'weaknesses of the flesh', the struggles and sorrows brought by our mortality. But more than that—even though he was innocent, Jesus actually died accursed, and descended into the grave.

If we did not have the apocalyptic view of reality brought by the resurrection, then at this point in the story we could be forgiven for thinking that Jesus was a sinner like the rest of us. The wages of sin is death, and after all, when he was hanging on the cross, dying under the curse of God, it certainly looked like Jesus was 'sinful flesh' like everyone else.[71]

But the resurrection changes our view of it all. If we remember the incarnation at Christmas, and the death of Jesus on Good Friday, Easter Day proclaims to the world that there has been a resurrection; a man has come back from the dead.

If Jesus is the centre of the central message of the New Testament, then his death and resurrection is the two-sided centre of the centre! His death is the way into the underworld, and his resurrection the way out.

According to the New Testament, three days after he died, they found his grave empty. His body had gone. Then he began appearing to people alive again, risen from the grave. After forty days of such appearances, 'proofs' that he was alive, he 'ascended' from the earth, as if he was floating into the clouds. On the great day of Pentecost, the Spirit of God was sent into the world after being expected for centuries, and Peter explained that this was because Jesus Christ had been exalted to the heavens and was now seated at the right hand of God, as

Lord of the universe. The writer to the Hebrews says that he had "passed through the heavens".[72]

Did you notice all the underworld spaces? It's as if Jesus has gone through them all to deal with them all. The victory he won on the cross, dying for the sins of the world, he then took with him to all the underworld spaces. And because he has 'come down', and 'gone back up'; because he has 'passed through the heavens', he has cleansed the whole universe. The underworld beings are now defeated and tamed, for now he is in the highest space, and all others must bow before him. As the rest of that early Christian hymn puts it:

> Therefore God has highly exalted him and bestowed
> on him the name that is above every name, so that at
> the name of Jesus every knee should bow, in heaven
> and on earth and under the earth, and every tongue
> confess that Jesus Christ is Lord, to the glory of God
> the Father. (Phil 2:9-11)

The resurrection unveils a completely new perspective on reality. It shows, for a start, that despite initial appearances, Jesus truly was innocent. The human courts put him to death as if he deserved it, but God's verdict overturns that human verdict. The resurrection declares to the world that Jesus didn't deserve to die at all. He really was the perfect human being.

If he was innocent, why did he die in the first place? This is where the news of Jesus is really good news. For in his death, he did not die for his own sins but for the sins of the world. When he died, he took the 'wages of sin' upon his own shoulders, and poured out his life "as a ransom for many".[73] In the words of Isaiah 53, he gave himself as an offering for sin. He died in order to deal with the *hamartia* that had ruined the rest of us.

It is here that the beauty of this strangest of all battles really strikes home. Goliath was a soldier who knew that battles are fought face to face, hand to hand, sword to sword. If it isn't one army against another, then it is one champion, one hero, against another. One champion defeats the other in one-on-one combat, and the rest of his people are the victors. Although he knew how the system worked, unfortunately for Goliath, a small boy brought his giant frame crashing down in a most remarkable way.

Jesus' victory over the prince and champion of the underworld was even more dramatic. I am not sure whether you have noticed, but so far in speaking about Jesus' victory, we have spoken about him dying on the cross for the sins of the world, and the resurrection showing that he was innocent, so that he is like an unblemished, sacrificial lamb. We have spoken of his death for our sin; his death bringing us forgiveness, salvation. But where is the devil in all that?

If we apply the Goliath school of warfare, we might have expected Jesus, our champion, to face off with the devil in some kind of cosmic head-to-head battle. He certainly spoke of this looming battle, as he moved towards the cross. In John 12, he declares that the hour has finally come: "Now is the judgment of this world; now will the ruler of this world be cast out".[74] But then what happened? He died on the cross as a ransom for many, and then he rose again from the grave to show that that ransom had achieved what it was meant to achieve. Forgiveness could now be proclaimed to the world. New life was available. God had loved the world and given his only Son. Now there was no need for anyone to perish anymore, because now anyone who believed in the Son could have eternal life. The victory was proclaimed, the spoils of battle distributed. But where in all of this was the hand-to-hand stoush between the prince of the underworld and the prince of life?

This is the strange twist of the story. Jesus defeated the devil well and truly, but he did so *by neutralizing his power over us*. There was no head-to-head. There was no cosmic clash of the titans. Jesus defeated the devil by dealing with our sin and God's wrath against it. As he went to his death, he reaffirmed that "the ruler of this world is coming. He has no claim on me …"[75] Jesus was innocent of any crime or sin, the only perfect human being ever, so of course the devil had no claim on him, no grounds for accusation. When Jesus died, he died to take our sins upon himself, "in his body on the tree" (that is, the cross).[76] He was the propitiation for our sins, the sacrifice that dealt with God's wrath.[77] And if our sins and our guilt and our punishment were all dealt with by the Son of God when he died on the cross, then there is nothing left for the Accuser to accuse us with. The devil's power is gone! He has no claim on us either. He has been neutralized.

> If God is for us, who can be against us? He who did not spare his own Son but gave him up for us all, how will he not also with him graciously give us all things? Who shall bring any charge against God's elect? It is God who justifies. Who is to condemn? Christ Jesus is the one who died—more than that, who was raised—who is at the right hand of God, who indeed is interceding for us. (Rom 8:31-34)

Jesus defeated the devil resoundingly and completely but in a sense *indirectly*. It was not as if there were two equal princes, arrayed against each other, slugging it out. The Son of God was above all that kind of thing. He defeated the devil by removing the problem that had enslaved us to him in the first place. He took away our guilt; he bore our punishment; he dealt with God's anger; he brought justification, that great declaration of innocence before the courtroom of God. And if God has looked at what his dear Son has won for us, and declared us to be 'not guilty', then the devil no longer has any hold over us. He has been defeated once and for all, without the Son of God ever having to stoop to direct confrontation with him at all.

When Jesus came back from the grave, and "passed through the heavens", it was so the world might know that the one who had the power of death had no power over the Lord Jesus Christ, no power at all. And this means that the power of the underworld has been thoroughly neutralized. The flawless hero has come, and he has won the victory on our behalf, once and for all time.

CHAPTER 7

A New Space in the Universe

*T*HE UNDERWORLD BELOW, the underworld above, the underworld all around. Jesus has passed through it all, bringing a true *catharsis*, a true cleansing. But his actions are finished, and external to us. They are *for* us, not *in* us. So how does his glorious victory out there in the real world help us with that basic human problem that lurks within *our* real world? How does the apocalyptic unveiling of cosmic reality from God's side help little old me? What about the underworld within? What about the beast that is there in Tony Soprano, Johnny Cash—and deep within you and me?

Speaking of beasts, if you are not a completely besotted Johnny Depp fan, *Fear and Loathing in Las Vegas* (1998) is one of those movies that leaves you at the end wondering if you really needed to see it. It documents the road to drug-induced self-destruction taken by journalist Raoul Duke (Depp, of course) and his attorney, Dr Gonzo. The novel on which the film was based was a largely fictionalized account of the 1971 experience of the author, 'gonzo journalist' Hunter S Thompson (who, sad to say, shot himself in February 2005). Strangely, the self-destruction portrayed in *Fear and Loathing* is supposed to point to a moment in history when the 1960s freedom movement, and then the hippy era, was riding the crest of a wave that was about to break and roll back out to sea. At one point, a line stands out as something of a motto for the film: "Man becomes a beast because he is too afraid to be a man".

Being a Bible reader, this reminded me of Psalm 49, where human beings are described as being "like the beasts that perish". The Bible story that we have been following so far is clear: human beings were not created to die; we had death thrust upon us. We sinned against our Creator, with the result that we now die. We were meant to shine out the glory of the immortal God, but instead, by our own doing, we now exist as mere mortals, dying like animals. And because we die like animals, we begin to live like animals—animals of the worst kind. We have become like beasts because we were too afraid to be human.

Once again, this is where the apocalyptic unveiling of reality is necessary to fully understand our situation. One of the writers in the Old Testament who reflected most on the problem of living with the underworld was 'the Preacher' of Ecclesiastes. He began his enterprise by trying to understand the world on its own terms, what he called 'under the sun'. As you looked around at this world, what could you observe about life? His results were what many would call 'glass-half-empty' thinking; others would describe it as 'sober realism'. At one point, he thinks about the old explanation of death as 'the body going downwards, the soul flying upwards', and asks, 'But how do you know?':

> I said in my heart with regard to the children of man that God is testing them that they may see that they themselves are but beasts. For what happens to the children of man and what happens to the beasts is the same; as one dies, so dies the other. They all have the same breath, and man has no advantage over the beasts, for all is vanity. All go to one place. All are from the dust, and to dust all return. Who knows whether the spirit of man goes upward and the spirit of the beast goes down into the earth? (Eccl 3:18-21)

This wasn't written in Las Vegas, but it could have been. The Preacher is clear. From observation 'under the sun', if we have no future but the grave, and no way of knowing what happens beyond it (if anything), then we are just like the beasts. And if we are just another two-legged form of animal, then where is the supposed glory of humanity? If we are beasts, we may as well live like beasts. Dog eat dog.

But when Jesus rose from the dead, that unveiling of reality told us that human beings do have a future; they are much more than beasts. They were born to be human, and human they can be. But without that apocalyptic perspective, life looks pretty grim for anyone who cares to think on it.

As I thought about the drug-fuelled, irrationally optimistic segment of American history that Hunter S Thompson was involved in and then wrote about, I thought about the rest of Psalm 49. It's just as poignant:

Man in his pomp will not remain;
    he is like the beasts that perish.
This is the path of those who have foolish
      confidence;
    yet after them people approve of their boasts.
Like sheep they are appointed for Sheol
      [the underworld];
    Death shall be their shepherd ...
Man in his pomp yet without understanding is like
      the beasts that perish. (Ps 49:12-14, 20)

Drugs may provide momentary *euphoria*, a feeling that all is well. And, as we have seen, the master of the underworld can provide any number of things in this world to encourage such feelings. But even in this life, we catch a glimpse of how empty the Deceiver's promises are—such as when we experience a drug-induced *dysphoria* (a bad trip, paranoid moment, schizoid attack, long-term addictive downslide), or when moments of clarity suddenly reveal to us the long-term damaging consequences of previous actions and patterns of behaviour. Satan offers a slavery that is ultimately destructive—and not just of brain cells, bodily functions and relationships. The underworld is all around us. Its darkness may be masked by loud music and chemicals, but the darkness is still there. The hippies reacted to Western consumerism (at least when they were young, before they settled down and became boomer consumers). And that was a good thing. For, as we have seen, consumerism by any other name is just a deceptive promise of security to those who are deeply disturbed by a core anxiety about death. But to react against consumerism by consuming chemicals and by 'becoming a beast'? Despite the grandiose world-changing dreams of a previous generation, as their legacy we now have *Fear and Loathing* in all kinds of cities and towns and countries—self-destruction for the sake of entertainment.

Man becomes a beast because he is too afraid to be a man—Hunter S Thompson.

Man in his pomp yet without understanding is like the beasts that perish—Psalm 49.

BUT.

For a small word, it has a lot of power. In contrast to the darkness into which we have descended; in contrast to the fear of death that has brought us into slavery; in contrast to the fear of being human that has turned us into beasts; in sharp contrast to the underworld that lies below, and above, and all around us, and whose master works his deception and destruction upon us through all the ordinary means—in contrast to all this, Jesus Christ has come, drawing back the curtain on reality from God's side, passing through all the underworld spaces, and dealing with all the underworld beings, especially its dark master. Jesus Christ has defeated the underworld by dying for the sins of the world, simultaneously dealing with our sin and with God's answering judgement upon that sin. Jesus Christ has risen from the dead, clearly demonstrating his victory over the underworld within human history in a way that speaks to all people in all places and for all times. If he has defeated our greatest enemy, then he has defeated all our enemies. He has come out of the grave, passed through the heavens, and is now seated as Lord, at the right hand of God the Father.

With its apocalyptic perspective on life, the gospel of Jesus Christ now proclaims a new way of living with the underworld. There is no need to succumb. There is a way of being rescued. There is a path back from the beasts, back towards being human again at last—in fact, for the very first time.

The journey towards being newly human begins with finding a new space that has opened up in the universe. In our increasingly addicted society, we are familiar with 'rehab', where Sandra Bullock spent *28 Days* (2000) on the screen, and many other stars can spend much more time off the screen. Rehab is a brief moment of safety, in which you are protected and shielded from the pressures (and suppliers and enablers) of everyday life. It is a safe-house. Such are the pressures and fears of Western society at the moment that 'safety' is rapidly becoming one of the chief virtues and goals to which we all aspire. If we can just have safe playgrounds, safe schools, safe work places, safe homes, safe equipment, safe everything, then life will be okay and we can breathe a sigh of relief, sit down ... and burn our lips on the coffee.

But if 'safety' only means protection from harm, then it is still a long way from being a virtue, or something that actually enhances our life. If rehab only provided safety and protection, then the stars would never go home, as they set up in this oasis for the rest of their mortal lives. Rehab knows that the beast lies within. It even tries to tame the beast within, with mixed success.

The new space God has opened up in the universe is certainly a place of safety, no doubt about that. But it is also a space of 'rest' and 'peace', filled with God's 'blessing'. Each of these biblical words speaks of positive, life-enhancing things—not just protection, but renovation, renewal, and life to the full. This new 'space' is actually a person, for the gospel of Jesus invites us to begin to live 'in him'. Jesus himself is the new 'space' in which we can become truly human.

Jesus himself began the call: "Come to me, all who labour and are heavy laden, and I will give you rest".[78] This metaphor of finding rest 'in Christ' goes back a long way. On that battlefield long ago, the giant Goliath was defeated by Israel's unexpected champion, the young shepherd boy David. David went on to become Israel's king—their king 'after God's own heart'. Because David was God's own choice, and because God had promised to be with him, Israel's only positive future was to be on David's side, and under his leadership and direction. Their only chance at being 'at rest' or 'at peace', prospering under God's blessing, was to be 'in David'.[79]

On another occasion, Jesus likened himself to a vine, and his people to its branches.[80] If the branches are cut off, they wither and die, but if they draw their nourishment from the vine, then they prosper and grow. Jesus used this metaphor to speak of the need for people to 'remain', or 'abide', or 'continue to live', 'in him'. He further explained that this would mean 'abiding in his love', and because his love is explained and revealed in the word of the gospel, he also spoke of 'abiding' in his words.

This is the language of incorporation. We are no longer treated in isolation, on our own, but as if we are connected to Jesus Christ. We are connected to Jesus Christ quite simply 'by faith' in him—that is, by putting our trust in him for God's forgiveness of our sins, for our salvation in the future, and for our life in the present. Finding this new 'space' is as easy as that—turning to Jesus Christ and trusting him with your life. And from the moment we are 'in Christ', all the benefits of his life, death and resurrection are granted to us.

But a branch doesn't join a vine and then leave again, if it wants to stay alive. In the same way, joining Christ is a lifetime thing. When the apostle Paul drew on this kind of imagery he clearly felt that being 'in Christ' was not just a brief jaunt to a place for a short-term stay. We should be found 'in Christ' throughout all of life. We should not just start in Christ, but continue in him:

> … as you received Christ Jesus the Lord, so walk in
> him, rooted and built up in him and established in
> the faith, just as you were taught, abounding in
> thanksgiving. (Col 2:6-7)

Paul loved this expression. He spoke over and over again of the privilege of being 'in Christ'. In Paul's writings it becomes clear that if we are 'in Christ', then from God's point of view, whatever happened to Jesus happened to us. So when he lived a perfect life, God regards us as having lived a perfect life. When he died on the cross, it was as if we died on the cross. When he died for sin, removing the wrath of God, it was *our* sin and our wrath he took. When he was buried, we were buried. When he descended to the underworld, we did too. And, then most amazingly, when he burst through the bonds of death, came out of the grave, rose from the dead, ascended into heaven and was seated at the right hand of the Father—can you believe it—so did we! Small wonder that those who have found this secure, restful place keep on "abounding in thanksgiving"! When we are located 'in Christ' by faith, living with the underworld looks very different indeed.

Now, of course, we are already familiar with spatial language being used metaphorically. To speak of being 'in Christ' does not mean that we are somehow literally 'in' the resurrected body of Jesus. But, as we have already seen, metaphor does not mean unreality. It helps us speak about aspects of reality that are, at least at the moment, beyond our ability to describe more exactly because they are not part of our first-hand experience. The 'in Christ' language speaks of reality—in fact, ultimate reality. It is speaking of reality as God now sees it. God says that, from his point of view, everything that Jesus did *for us* is credited to our account, as if we had done it all too. And if this is reality 'as God sees it', then it *is* reality and it *always will be* reality. He will never let us go. Not only are we 'in Christ', but, as Jesus put it, we are safe in his hand, and in the Father's hand:

> "My sheep hear my voice, and I know them, and they
> follow me. I give them eternal life, and they will
> never perish, and no one will snatch them out of my
> hand. My Father, who has given them to me, is
> greater than all, and no one is able to snatch them
> out of the Father's hand. I and the Father are one."
> (John 10:27-30)

But if this is the way God sees things, then this is the way we should see things too, because this is our future; this is what will be the case one day. God has promised, and therefore it will be done. And notice how this 'space' is directly answering all the fears of the underworld. For those in Christ, this is a place of safety and protection, a place of rest and security. And it is a security that will survive even the grave, for Jesus gives his 'sheep' eternal life so that they will not perish, and he promises that nothing will prevent them from being raised up on the future resurrection day:

> "All that the Father gives me will come to me, and whoever comes to me I will never cast out. For I have come down from heaven, not to do my own will but the will of him who sent me. And this is the will of him who sent me, that I should lose nothing of all that he has given me, but raise it up on the last day. For this is the will of my Father, that everyone who looks on the Son and believes in him should have eternal life, and I will raise him up on the last day." (John 6:37-40)

What a wonderful new 'space' has been opened up for all of us, as we live on the thin strip of ground with the underworld on all sides! The apostle Paul was so moved by his own 'discovery' of this clearing in the darkness, that he could say: "Therefore, since we have been justified by faith, we have peace with God through our Lord Jesus Christ. Through him we have also obtained access by faith into this grace in which we stand, and we rejoice in hope of the glory of God".[81] This new 'space' is filled with God's grace, his generosity, his love.

Whereas once life was lived with a profound anxiety about the grave, eating away at our core, and so corrupting life in so many destructive ways, those in this new space have a *new core*. Instead of anxiety about death, they have an assurance about eternal life. This assurance doesn't take us away from all the sufferings of this world—at least, not until God's new creation arrives—but it brings us a deep peace that enables us to live in a new way in the midst of the sufferings of this world, whatever they might be. The underworld may cast its shadow still, but those 'in Christ' now live by a light that pierces the darkness, with a future that is absolutely guaranteed. And so "we rejoice in hope of the glory of God".

When Paul rejoices in the glory of God, he has a concrete reality in mind. Later in Romans he says:

> For I consider that the sufferings of this present time are not worth comparing with the glory that is to be revealed to us. For the creation waits with eager longing for the revealing of the sons of God. For the creation was subjected to futility, not willingly, but because of him who subjected it, in hope that the creation itself will be set free from its bondage to decay and obtain the freedom of the glory of the children of God. For we know that the whole creation has been groaning together in the pains of childbirth until now. And not only the creation, but we ourselves, who have the firstfruits of the Spirit, groan inwardly as we wait eagerly for adoption as sons, the redemption of our bodies. (Rom 8:18-23)

Before Christ came, we human beings had no future at all, apart from a grave in which our body would rot and decay. And although we may not have realized it, beyond the grave we also faced the fearful prospect of God's judgement and an eternity bearing his punishment for our sins. This black future cast its shadow back on all of our life. But now a new space has opened up, and for those who are 'in Christ' God has provided a glorious future, which will even include the resurrection of our bodies!

What happened to Jesus will happen to us too. It will happen to us, because it happened to Jesus, and everything that Jesus did was for us. This connection between Christ and those 'in Christ' is so rock solid, so firmly anchored in God's way of seeing things, that the New Testament speaks of it being a reality already. One of the most dramatic of these passages is in Paul's letter to the Colossians:

> If then you have been raised with Christ, seek the things that are above, where Christ is, seated at the right hand of God. Set your minds on things that are above, not on things that are on earth. For you have died, and your life is hidden with Christ in God. When Christ who is your life appears, then you also will appear with him in glory. (Col 3:1-4)

Our connection with Christ's death and resurrection is so real that Paul can say that "you have died, and your life is hidden with Christ in God". To be 'in Christ' is to be 'in God'; to be 'in Christ' is to be in heaven already! So much so, that when Jesus returns to wrap up the whole show and bring in God's new creation, Paul says that "you also will appear with him in glory". At that moment, for the first time, we will see ourselves for who we really are. Now that is an amazing thought that we will have to come back to.

All this talk of 'setting your mind on the things above', and meeting up with your heavenly self when Jesus returns, brings us to something else that is new, now that Jesus Christ has unveiled ultimate reality.

CHAPTER 8

Living with the Underworld

*A*BOUT FIFTY DAYS AFTER Jesus' resurrection, a dramatic event occurred in Jerusalem, witnessed by crowds of people from all over the world who happened to be in the city for the religious festival of Pentecost. There were people there who spoke many different languages. Suddenly, they heard the sound of a rushing wind, and as Jesus' Galilean disciples spoke about Jesus, each person in the crowd heard the words in his or her own native language.

Some wag in the crowd said it was because the disciples were drunk. (I have heard plenty of Australians with too much drink in them talking in strange ways, but I always thought it was the language of a pickled brain, not another country.) When the apostle Peter stood up to give an explanation, he said it was only 9 am, and so much too early for them to be drunk—must have been in the days before the 'early openers', or all night clubs. The real explanation for the rushing wind and the linguistic miracle was out of this world: despite being crucified and buried, Jesus had risen from the dead, passed through the heavens, and was now installed in heaven at the right hand of the Father. From this position of authority and power, he had received the promised Spirit of God, and 'poured out' the Spirit amongst his followers.

The New Testament has a lot to say about the Spirit— that is, God's own presence living with his people. There are certainly more questions and mysteries here, and much to say in response. But the most basic feature of the Spirit is that he is the Spirit of the future. This is not surprising, because not only was the pouring out of the Spirit the final act in Jesus' own resurrection, declaring his true position as Messiah and Son of God,[82] but the Spirit poured out by Jesus is also called "the Spirit of him who raised Jesus from the dead".[83] If love and marriage go together like peas and cabbage, the Spirit and the resurrection go together like tomato sauce and sausages at an Aussie BBQ.

This connection of the Spirit with the future is often missed, with the result that the Spirit is made to serve some cause which promotes security in terms of this present world. Some have tied the Spirit in with a certain Christian church or denomination, saying that the Spirit is now found there and its ministers are his mouthpieces. This means that the ordinary person gets in touch with the Spirit through being a member of that denomination and abiding by its rules. Closely related to this first view, the Spirit has also been tied in with certain kinds of rituals, so that the ordinary person experiences the Spirit through participation in these ceremonies. In recent days there has been an inordinate focus upon the extraordinary gifts that the Spirit is said to impart, so that people can be sure of the Spirit's presence because they have experienced these gifts in their lives.

Each of these views causes a person's security to be placed in some kind of experience (whether membership or ritual or 'charismatic'), and although the experiences themselves may be different, they each have the same focus: something in this present world. After thinking about the devil being given all the authority of the kingdoms of this world and their glory, this should alarm us. It is the prince of this world that wants us to find security in the things of this world. Perhaps the old '90% rule' is in operation here as well. If the devil can use something that looks almost like what the New Testament teaches, then that is another opportunity for the angel of light to deceive and gain a few 'nice little earners'. If he can take the Spirit of the future and turn him into the Spirit of the present, and he himself rules the present—bewdiful! And we are back to our slavery.

The New Testament portrays the Spirit as the Spirit of the future, the Spirit of resurrection. The people of Israel longed for the day when God's Spirit would be given to them all,[84] and their prophets promised that one day that would be the case.[85] On the extraordinary day of Pentecost in Jerusalem, these promises came to their moment of fulfilment when the risen, ascended Jesus poured out God's Spirit on his people. This was the Spirit of 'the age to come', which is why Peter could say that this event marked the arrival of the last days.[86]

The Spirit brought the future into this world. Paul described the Spirit as a 'deposit' or a 'guarantee',[87] the "guarantee of our inheritance until we acquire possession of it".[88] Just as a new home owner puts a deposit down to guarantee the full purchase in the future, so too God has put his deposit down to guarantee the fullness of his salvation in the future.

Paul also uses the agricultural/sacrificial metaphor of 'the firstfruits' to make the same point. In ancient Israel, when the first part of the harvest arrived, these firstfruits were to be offered to God. They were taken as a sign that the whole harvest was about to come in. So too, Jesus' resurrection was 'the firstfruits' of the resurrection harvest still to come.[89] Or, to say the same thing another way, since the Spirit and resurrection go together so closely, Paul could say that Christian people now have "the firstfruits of the Spirit", which makes them long for the day of resurrection, the redemption of our bodies.[90] The Spirit is the Spirit of the future.

This means that when the New Testament calls upon people to live by the Spirit, it is a call to live for the future—the future age and the future redemption of our bodies. As Paul says in Romans 8, we all begin with a mind set on the flesh,[91] subject to the law of sin and death.[92] This mind set on the flesh is hostile to God, and it cannot please God.[93] With everyone's mind set on the flesh, we live in a world of suffering.[94] This is where we all begin. Human beings begin life with a 'mind set on the flesh'—that is, we think from within the framework set by our mortal existence. That is why we end up enslaved to the desires of our bodies.

But once Jesus gives us the future back, everything

changes. He has so thoroughly dealt with our sin on the cross that there is "now no condemnation for those who are in Christ Jesus".[95] Those who are 'in Christ' now have their minds set on the Spirit—that is, we live with an eye on the resurrection day. All Christians have God's Spirit within them,[96] taking us out of the realm of the flesh into the realm of the Spirit. This is the Spirit of resurrection, which will raise Christ's people from the dead on the great day of resurrection.[97] We now have a real, concrete hope, and that hope will not disappoint us.

As a result of this new future, the New Testament contains any number of exhortations like that of Colossians 3:1-4, calling upon people to live as those who have a guaranteed standing as citizens of God's heavenly kingdom.[98] God sees those 'in Christ' as having died with Christ and risen again, and so this is how we should see ourselves: "consider yourselves dead to sin and alive to God in Christ Jesus";[99] "present yourselves to God as those who have been brought from death to life".[100] This is also behind the metaphor of 'changing clothes' that keeps cropping up in Paul's letters, where he exhorts his readers to 'put off' the old clothes of the flesh and put on the new clothes of the future.[101]

But these exhortations to live the future life even now should not be read within a moralistic framework which assumes we have the power to do so. The exhortation is given to people who have first been given the Spirit. This means we are not left to our own devices to make such momentous changes. There is a new force for change who actually lives within us, the Spirit of God. And as a fruit tree naturally grows fruit, the Spirit's fruit begins to be seen in our lives.[102]

The Spirit is the secret of the new heart. With the Spirit of God shaping our minds according to the future resurrection, we are given a new heart. The beast begins to be tamed. The love of God is poured into our hearts by the Spirit, as he teaches us about Jesus Christ's finished work on our behalf.[103] With our heart focused on Jesus and the resurrection, we see more than the grave. We see Jesus and the promise of eternal life. And as we see it, waiting for us beyond the grave, we long for that day of redemption. The whole world is groaning towards that day, and as the Spirit does his work on us, so we 'groan' towards that day, longing for the resurrection life of God's new creation.[104]

This basic change of mind and heart leads to a change of attitudes and values, and a new way of seeing everything in this world as we firmly set our minds on the next. We are no longer seeking after security in this world through following the desires of the body. Instead, we are secure about the next world, and so we live in this body in a new way, as we await its redemption.

There is tremendous assurance here. If the old life was an unbroken sequence of death and anxiety about death, leading to slavery, the new life is resurrection, assurance and freedom. This assurance abounds in the New Testament, but nowhere can surpass the final part of Romans 8. Here the underworld spaces and underworld beings are paraded before the readers' eyes, as we are told that nothing, anywhere in the universe, can separate those who are in Christ Jesus from the love of God in him:

> Who shall separate us from the love of Christ? Shall tribulation, or distress, or persecution, or famine, or nakedness, or danger, or sword? As it is written,

"For your sake we are being killed all the day
long;
we are regarded as sheep to be slaughtered."

No, in all these things we are more than conquerors
through him who loved us. For I am sure that neither
death nor life, nor angels nor rulers, nor things
present nor things to come, nor powers, nor height
nor depth, nor anything else in all creation, will be
able to separate us from the love of God in Christ
Jesus our Lord. (Rom 8:35-39)

If the love of Christ is ours, there is no need to fear—no
need to fear death; no need to fear the moment we enter
the underworld; no need to fear the underworld spaces;
no need to fear the beings we may or may not meet in
them. The love of God is ours in Christ, and nothing
and nobody can separate us from that love. With that
love, we have a guaranteed inheritance, raised from the
dead, into the kingdom of God, the new creation, glory
without pain. This will be our glorious day of liberty at
last—free to live forever!

The assurance is strong, but it needs to be, because
in the time before the resurrection day, those 'in Christ'
will have a particularly difficult time.

WE HAVE ALREADY SPOKEN OF THE SUFFERINGS OF
this world under the shadow of death. Living with the
underworld will continue to bring its pains for those 'in
Christ', because they are not taken out of the world
immediately when they put their faith in Jesus. They will
not be immune from the general sufferings of a dying

world. In fact, the New Testament specifically says that troubles, trials and sufferings are part of God's plan for us.

Think about it: the Spirit is working within our hearts so that we long for the day of resurrection. That means that our comfortable attachment to this world will be changing. We will no longer strive for security in the things of this world under Satan's domain, but resting secure 'in Christ' and his finished work on the cross for us, we will long for the ultimate security of God's new creation. That's why God doesn't spare us the trials and sufferings of life in this world, surrounded as it is by the underworld. The trials and sufferings perform an important function: they produce in us the Christian character that longs for the new creation, and the redemption of our bodies:

> Therefore, since we have been justified by faith, we have peace with God through our Lord Jesus Christ. Through him we have also obtained access by faith into this grace in which we stand, and we rejoice in hope of the glory of God. More than that, we rejoice in our sufferings, knowing that suffering produces endurance, and endurance produces character, and character produces hope, and hope does not put us to shame, because God's love has been poured into our hearts through the Holy Spirit who has been given to us. (Rom 5:1-5)

But the unveiling of reality in Jesus also shows us something that will make our situation worse. When Jesus dealt with our sin and God's answering judgement, when he died to take the wrath of God away from us, that made the master of the underworld hopping mad! This is described for us in the apocalyptic language of the last book in the Bible, the Book of Revelation. Here the devil is pictured as trying to destroy God's Messiah, but he fails to do so, because Christ is snatched up into heaven and kept safe.[105] So what does the enemy do then? Listen to the warning: "... woe to you, O earth and sea, for the devil has come down to you in great wrath, because he knows that his time is short!"[106] When he saw that the Messiah had been kept safe, "[t]hen the dragon became furious with the woman and went off to make war on the rest of her offspring, on those who keep the commandments of God and hold to the testimony of Jesus".[107] The Christ is taken to heaven, so the devil turns his anger against Christ's people. And he is furious, because he knows his time is short.

The brevity of the time has nothing to do with him. When Jesus rose from the dead and then poured out the Spirit, you will recall, this began "the last days".[108] God's centuries-long plan to reverse the effects of Adam's fall and to overcome the problem of death had come to a head and been completed. Jesus' finished work has begun the last days. This is the persistent teaching of the New Testament. We live in the last days. In fact, we live in the last hour.[109] The only reason that Christ has not returned, bringing the day of resurrection and the glorious kingdom of God, is that he wants people to turn back to him, to put their faith in him, to be found in that one true 'safe-house'—to be found, in other words, 'in him'.[110]

But if the times are short, then the devil knows his time is limited. He turns his anger on God's people. The New Testament warns us on several occasions to remember that the devil is around:

[G]ive no opportunity to *the devil*. (Eph 4:27)

Put on the whole armor of God, that you may be able to stand against the schemes of *the devil*. (Eph 6:11)

Submit yourselves therefore to God. Resist *the devil*, and he will flee from you. (Jas 4:7)

Be sober-minded; be watchful. Your adversary *the devil* prowls around like a roaring lion, seeking someone to devour. Resist him, firm in your faith, knowing that the same kinds of suffering are being experienced by your brotherhood throughout the world. (1 Pet 5:8-9)

But interestingly, while warning us about the devil, the New Testament doesn't make much of a fuss about it. In this brief time before the resurrection day, we are certainly engaged in a spiritual warfare, but the decisive battle has already been won by the Son of God on the cross. "It is finished" always applies, and so does "he has no claim on me".[111] The spiritual warfare now consists of holding onto our secure salvation, standing firm in our faith, preaching the gospel, and praying.[112]

What will this 'spiritual warfare' mean for us, day by day? What should we do? How should we prepare?

Let us begin with one thing that this certainly does *not* mean. Christians are never called upon to directly engage with the devil and his forces. There is no exhortation in the New Testament for anyone to perform exorcisms. In fact, the only passage that speaks of 'spiritual warfare' directly—Ephesians 6:10-20 —doesn't mention anything remotely like exorcism. What it mentions is what you might call the 'ordinary' things of the Christian life: faith, salvation, gospel preaching and prayer.

But, some might say, didn't Jesus do exorcisms? And, of course, he did. But we must remember that, unlike many philosophies and religions, the Christian movement is an historical faith. We proclaim that certain things happened in the past in connection with the coming of the Messiah that are complete and done and unrepeatable (because there is only one Messiah). We are not the Son of God. We don't continue to do Christ's ministry. We receive what he has done on our behalf, once and for all time.

But, some might then say, doesn't the risen Christ continue to do his work through us? And so shouldn't we expect him to continue to do exorcisms through us today? This misunderstands the finished work of Christ. The risen Christ does not continue to do the same kinds of things he did when he walked this earth. When he arrived in this world the forces of evil rose up against him, and when they did, he dealt with them. But at that stage, the main battleground still lay ahead of him. By his initiative, and according to God's eternal plan of the ages, he would lay down his life and defeat the devil in that strangest of all battles, on the cross. Jesus dealt with our sin, and God's wrath against our sin, and thus completely obliterated any power the devil might have over us. As it says in Revelation 12:11: "And they have conquered him [the dragon] by the blood of the Lamb and by the word of their testimony". Jesus didn't directly fight the devil in hand-to-hand spiritual warfare. He drew his sting, and left him powerless. There was no direct engagement by Jesus, and there is none called for from his people.

And once his work on the cross was finished, it was finished! He then "sat down at the right hand of God".[113] The only thing left to do is for the finished work of Christ to be proclaimed to the nations so that it can be heard, and believed, so that (as that banner shouts so loudly from the grandstand) "whoever believes in him should not perish, but have eternal life".

But, some might say, even if we cannot or should not imitate our Lord's exorcisms, perhaps we should continue to do exorcisms because Jesus' disciples did. Once again, we should remember that Christianity is an historical faith. The Gospels and Acts tell us what the apostles did in history, not what every Christian (or any Christian) should necessarily continue to do for all time after that special apostolic period. Of course, there are some things that both Jesus and the apostles did that we *should* imitate—laying down our lives in love for the sake of other people, for example.[114] So how do we know which aspects are unique to Jesus and the apostles, and which aspects we should consciously repeat or imitate?

That's what the epistles of the New Testament are for. In letter after letter, the apostles deal with the real lives and struggles of the first Christian churches— teaching and reminding them about the gospel and teasing out its implications for their lives, rebuking their errors, applauding their successes, urging them to persevere, answering their questions, and challenging their ungodliness. It's in the epistles that we find the shape of the Christian life described, its challenges outlined, its goals and nature defined. And in the epistles we find absolutely no expectation or command that Christians should be doing exorcisms. Not a mention. Not even a hint that this is something the apostles expected Christian churches to be involved in.

This shouldn't surprise us. The apostles were a select, specially chosen group (as were the 72 in Luke 10), and they had a special foundational role in the Christian movement. They performed various extraordinary deeds as an indication that they were, in fact, specially authorized as Christ's apostles—"the signs of a true apostle" as Paul calls them.[115] They did not expect all Christians to do these things or perform these signs—in fact, these signs wouldn't have been signs of an apostle if everyone could do them.

The New Testament gives absolutely no encouragement to Christians to directly engage with the devil or demons through such practices as exorcism or deliverance or praying against territorial spirits. This must be stressed, because over the last 40 years or so a number of movements have arisen within the Christian orbit urging exactly this kind of direct engagement with the devil and his minions. There are exorcism ministries, and deliverance ministries, some even claiming that this kind of thing ought to form a regular part of congregational life. Please forgive me for speaking strongly, but love requires that a clear message be heard: these 'ministries' are not Christian ministries in the New Testament sense. They are profoundly misguided, and should be shut down, never to be re-opened.

One very important clue that these ministries are not truly Christian ministries is that they reintroduce the fear of the underworld that Jesus died to banish. The ancient world was afraid to step in the wrong spot in case they came across an underworld space, or an underworld being, that then worked evil upon their lives and families. Everybody was afraid of the curses of magic that were used to inflict such underworld pain. But Jesus died, descended into the underworld, rose again, passed through the heavens and is now seated far above any underworld space or any underworld being, and why? For the church. For us. There is no need to fear anymore:

> There is no fear in love, but perfect love casts out fear. For fear has to do with punishment, and whoever fears has not been perfected in love. (1 John 4:18)

> For you did not receive the spirit of slavery to fall back into fear, but you have received the Spirit of adoption as sons, by whom we cry, "Abba! Father!" (Rom 8:15)

So why do these ministries scare the life out of people once again? Why are we warned that we could be under a curse, afflicted upon us by some ancestor's involvement in a Masonic order, or through someone else being involved in the occult? Why are we told that we can accidentally, imperceptibly 'give the devil a foothold', to misquote Ephesians 4:27, which is taken to mean giving the devil an opportunity to take possession of your body, or to seriously influence your life for the worse? (Instead, the verse is saying that anger against a Christian brother harms the life and unity of God's people, which is what the devil is also trying to do—so why help him along in his mission? We should be serving Jesus' mission.)

We have received a Spirit of sonship that breathes the comfort of the gospel into our souls. Jesus has taken hold of us, and nobody can snatch us out of his or the

Father's hands. We are secure, we are loved, we have a future, and all of this means: *no more fear*. Why, then, would we put people through some dreadful, dramatic experience, said to be a demonic expulsion, so that from then on they look back in fear and say, "But what really happened back then?" If any ministry claims to be Christian and raises the old fears again, then it is seriously misguided and is not being governed by the gospel of God's grace. And I repeat my strong words: such ministries should be disbanded, for they are doing nothing good for the work of Christ in this world and, in fact, are doing harm. Those involved may be well-meaning and wanting to help, and their ministries may be dressed up with all kinds of other helpful Christian teaching, but to create fear is not the work of God. It is unwittingly to play into the devil's hands, because fear has always been one of his favourite instruments (remember Hebrews 2:14-15).

THE CHRISTIAN FIGHT TAKES PLACE WITH DIFFERENT weapons and a different strategy. Our weapon is the gospel of Christ, and our strategy is to remember it, speak it, believe it, cling to it and pray in response to it! It may seem very different from the weapons and warfare of this world, but that's good—remember who owns this world! If we are attracted to dramatic, direct encounters with the world of evil because their dramatic, direct nature seems to suggest great power, then we should beware. This is very likely a 'weapon of this world' dressed up in a 'spiritual' disguise. The gospel will always look weak and helpless. What is 'a mere word' against such displays of power? What are a few mumbled prayers given in normal human language compared with dramatic spiritual pyrotechnics? But these are our true and only spiritual weapons. Our spiritual warfare begins and ends by the gospel reminding us of Jesus' victory. Whatever we are facing, whatever fears afflict our soul, we are to remember Jesus' victory on our behalf.

This ought to bring us deep assurance. The ancient magicians believed that in order to control the spirits they had to name them. This took them into the very dangerous game of direct engagement with the underworld. But the gospel of Jesus makes this completely unnecessary. Whatever beasts are out there— whatever ghosts and ghoulies, demons and devils, spooks and spirits, principalities and powers—we don't need to name them, speak to them, or give them the honour of a token thought. In fact, it would be misguided to do so. All we need to do is to remember the gospel, believe the gospel, rejoice in the gospel, thank God for the gospel, and proclaim the gospel, over and over again. For that gospel tells us of Christ's once-and-for-all victory. Through his death and resurrection, Jesus Christ has been placed over every single one of the underworld beings that have existed, or may exist, or may not exist except in our fearful imagination! He has extinguished the devil's power, so that he has no claim on us. There is no need to fear any more. Jesus has the victory, and we are in Christ.

How, then, do we 'resist the devil'? Not by turning to face him, but by turning to face Christ; not by engaging directly with him, but by engaging directly with

Christ in his gospel. We resist him by standing firm, fixing our eyes on Jesus, and letting the devil go to his absolutely certain fate. If we resist in this Christ-centred way, the promise of the Scriptures is so clear and so easy: he will flee from you.[116] He is a defeated enemy. Let's leave him that way, and not treat him as if he still has any claim on our lives.

Perhaps the most damaging consequence of focusing on exorcism, deliverance, and other dramatic forms of so-called 'spiritual warfare' is that it diverts our attention from the truth that is so clearly observed in the Scriptures: Satan works through very ordinary means. His attacks come with an everyday plausibility and a reassuring smile, not with green vomit and spinning heads (as in *The Exorcist*). By God's permission, the whole world is the devil's and so his attacks come through the world and its attractiveness.

A distinction has often been made between Satan's external and internal attacks. The external would be things like persecution at the hands of governments or bosses. The internal is the 'temptation to sin'. But it is best to see the devil's work as external. Satan uses the circumstances and opportunities of this world to lead our weak, beastly hearts astray. Even as Christians we will continue to face these attacks, because the renovation of our hearts will not be complete until the resurrection day. Our hearts will continue to long for security, and we will continue to be dazzled and attracted by all this world has to offer to provide that security. The devil will continue to promise satisfaction for our troubled hearts through the ordinary means of wealth, possessions, pleasure, sexual immorality, pride, status, reputation, education, experience, family and societal connections, power and the like—all the things that give us a firm stake in this world, that help us to get ahead.

We resist these lies of the devil by holding onto the truth of Christ's victory, and then pressing on to live the resurrection life now. And it is another amazing thing about New Testament 'spirituality' that when it describes the Spirit-empowered life we are to live now, it keeps going on about ordinary life—such as in the various 'household codes', in which readers are told how to put on the life of the resurrection.[117] In these passages, husbands and wives are told how to treat each other; parents and children too. There are encouragements and instructions for slaves and masters, and citizens and governments. The life of the Spirit sends us back into human relationships as transformed people. We are no longer trying to solve our death-anxiety by using and abusing others, or by competing with them to win. Instead, by being 'in Christ' we have defeated death and been raised from the dead, and so we seek to love others, even as we have been so greatly loved. Once the underworld problem is solved, the beast within begins to stop its baying, and a true human begins to emerge.

According to Hunter S Thompson, we are afraid to be human, and so we become beasts. According to the Bible, we are afraid of death and so we become beasts. But 'in Christ' there is no more to fear, and we can now begin to become truly human. This all comes from having a secure home, a place of rest for eternity. Outside of Christ, our only prospect was a rotten grave and an eternity under God's judgement. Now, in Christ, we look forward to the end of the underworld, where the dark spaces and the dark beings will at last be destroyed. Jesus' victory on the cross will be applied to every corner of the universe. Death and Hades will be "thrown into the lake of fire", along with the devil and all his messengers.[118] There will be (in more picture language) a "new heaven and a new earth" and a "new Jerusalem".[119] There will be those who are excluded from this renovation of all things—but only those who have excluded themselves by refusing to be joined to Jesus Christ and so to find safety and blessing 'in him'. This exclusion is God's punishment in God's properly ordered new world. But there is no need for anyone to suffer that kind of dreadful eternity. Remember our sporting enthusiast: "God so loved the world [i.e. *you*], that he gave his only Son, that whoever believes in him [i.e. *you*] should not perish but have eternal life".

At last there is no need to be afraid of death or eternity, and in your fear to end up like a beast. There is no need to fear underworld spaces, or beings, or even the underworld Master, because the underworld problem has been dealt with once and for all. Jesus died for us so that we might live for him, and those who live for him (and 'in him') will live forever![120] This deep assurance and peace frees us up to be human beings, for the first time in our entire pathetic existence. The old pattern was: death, anxiety and slavery. But the new pattern is: resurrection, assurance and freedom. And if the Son shall set you free, you shall be free indeed.

ENDNOTES

1. Matthew 11:19
2. Matthew 15:1-20
3. Matthew 23:27
4. Luke 8:31
5. John 3:13, 31; 17:11; Mark 14:62
6. Ephesians 4:9-11; cf. Romans 10:7
7. 1 Peter 3:19-20; Ephesians 4:8
8. Mark 9:48; Rev 19:20; Luke 16:23-24
9. Ephesians 2:2, 6:12; 2 Corinthians 12:2
10. Philippians 2:10
11. Matthew 15:1-20
12. Psalm 49:11
13. "There is no-one who does not fear to be spellbound by curse tablets" (Pliny, *Natural History*, 28.4.19).
14. The Greek festival of Anthesteria and the Roman festivals of Lemuria and Parentalia (which concluded with Feralia) involved sacrifices to appease the spirits of the dead.
15. Mark 5:9
16. 'Will sue to avoid goblins', *Aftenposten*, 29 November 2006: http://www.aftenposten.no/english/local/article1550511.ece
17. John van Tiggelen, 'Who You Gonna Call?', *Good Weekend*, 6 January 2007.
18. Acts 19:11-20
19. Only eight times, to be exact: Matthew 12:45; Luke 7:21, 8:2, 11:26; Acts 19:12, 13, 15, 16.
20. Translated literally, the Greek of Mark 1:23 says: "And immediately in their synagogue there was a man *in an unclean spirit*, and he cried out ..."

21. Mark 3:22
22. Mark 1:24
23. *Sydney Morning Herald*, 2-3 February 2002.
24. John 8:44; Acts 3:15
25. 1 John 3:8
26. John 8:44
27. 2 Timothy 2:26
28. Luke 4:6
29. Matthew 28:18
30. John 12:31
31. 2 Corinthians 4:4
32. Revelation 12:9; 1 John 5:19
33. 2 Corinthians 11:14
34. Mark 8:27-33
35. Psalm 14:1
36. Genesis 11:4
37. e.g. Mark 4:15
38. Genesis 3:6
39. 1 Samuel 17
40. Mark 3:27
41. John 12:31
42. Epictetus, *The Discourses,* IV.i.
43. John 11:33, 35, 38
44. Luke 19:10
45. John 3:16
46. Romans 6:23
47. Genesis 2:17
48. Romans 5:12
49. Genesis 5
50. See Genesis 5:5, 8, 11, 14, 17, 20, etc.
51. Job 18:14
52. Matthew 4:8
53. e.g. Psalm 69:15
54. Psalm 49:7-9
55. Romans 6:12
56. John 19:30
57. 1 Peter 1:3
58. e.g. Matthew 10:34; John 3:19, 12:46
59. e.g. Matthew 10:40; Luke 4:18; John 4:34
60. e.g. Hebrews 9:26; 1 John 3:8
61. John 1:14
62. Acts 2:27-31 quotes and comments upon Psalm 16 to say that
    although, like David, Jesus went to the dead (i.e. Hades), unlike

David he didn't stay there; he wasn't "abandoned" there to see corruption.

63. Romans 10:7
64. Hebrews 10:5
65. Hebrews 2:14
66. Hebrews 5:8
67. Hebrews 4:15
68. Athanasius writes: "In addition, if the enemy of our race, the devil, having fallen from heaven moves around in this lower atmosphere, and lording it here over his fellow demons in disobedience, through them works vain fancies to cheat man and tries to prevent them from rising upwards, the Apostle speaks of this also: 'According to the ruler of the power of the air, who now works in the sons of disobedience'. But the Lord came to overthrow the devil, purify the air, and open for us the way up to heaven, as the Apostle said, 'through the veil, that is, his flesh'. This had to be effected by death, and by what other death would these things have been accomplished save by that which takes place in the air, I mean the cross? For only he who expires on the cross dies in the air. So it was right for the Lord to endure it. For being raised up in this way he purified the air from the wiles of the devil and all demons, saying: 'I saw Satan falling as lightning'. And he opened the way up to heaven ..." (On the Incarnation, 25).
69. Ephesians 4:8; I Peter 3:19-20
70. Romans 10:7
71. See Romans 8:3
72. Hebrews 4:14
73. Mark 10:45
74. John 12:31
75. John 14:30
76. I Peter 2:24
77. Romans 3:24-25
78. Matthew 11:28
79. 2 Samuel 19:43-20:1
80. John 15:1-11
81. Romans 5:1-2
82. See Acts 2:32-36; Romans 1:4
83. Romans 8:11
84. Numbers 11:29
85. Joel 2:28-32
86. Acts 2:16-17
87. 2 Corinthians 1:22
88. Ephesians 1:14

89. 1 Corinthians 15:20, 23
90. Romans 8:23
91. Romans 8:6a
92. Romans 8:2
93. Romans 8:7-8
94. Romans 8:18, 22
95. Romans 8:1
96. Romans 8:9
97. Romans 8:11, 23
98. e.g. Ephesians 2:4-10; Philippians 3:17-4:1; 1 John 3:1-3
99. Romans 6:11
100. Romans 6:13
101. See Ephesians 4:22-24; Colossians 3:5-17; Romans 13:12-14
102. Galatians 5:22-24
103. Romans 5:5-8
104. Romans 8:23-25
105. Revelation 12
106. Revelation 12:12
107. Revelation 12:17
108. Acts 2:16-17
109. 1 John 2:18
110. Romans 2:4; 2 Peter 3:8-9
111. John 19:30; 14:30
112. See how this is spelled out in Ephesians 6:10-20.
113. Hebrews 10:12
114. 1 John 3:16; Ephesians 4:32-5:1
115. 2 Corinthians 12:12
116. James 4:7
117. Ephesians 5:15-6:9; Colossians 3:18-4:6; 1 Peter 2:11-3:12
118. Revelation 20:14; Matthew 25:41
119. Revelation 21:1-2
120. 2 Corinthians 5:15

Matthias Media is a ministry team of like-minded, evangelical Christians working together to achieve a particular goal, as summarized in our mission statement:

> *To serve our Lord Jesus Christ, and the growth of his gospel in the world, by producing and delivering high quality, Bible-based resources.*

It was in 1988 that we first started pursuing this mission together, and in God's kindness we now have more than 250 different ministry resources being distributed all over the world. These resources range from Bible studies and books, through to training courses and audio sermons.

To find out more about our large range of very useful products, and to access samples and free downloads, visit our website:

www.matthiasmedia.com.au

How to buy our resources

1. Direct from us over the internet:
   – in the US: www.matthiasmedia.com
   – in Australia and the rest of the world: www.matthiasmedia.com.au

2. Direct from us by phone:
   – in the US: 1 866 407 4530
   – in Australia: 1800 814 360 (Sydney: 9663 1478)
   – international: +61-2-9663-1478

3. Through a range of outlets in various parts of the world. Visit **www.matthiasmedia.com.au/international.php** for details about recommended retailers in your part of the world, including www.thegoodbook.co.uk in the United Kingdom.

4. Trade enquiries can be addressed to:
   – in the US: sales@matthiasmedia.com
   – in the UK: sales@ivpbooks.com
   – in Australia and the rest of the world: sales@matthiasmedia.com.au

Also from Matthias Media

Guidebooks for Life
Bible-based essentials for your Christian journey

Some Christian books are all theory and no practical application; others are all stories and tips with no substance. The Guidebooks for Life series aims to achieve a vital balance—that is, to dig into the Bible and discover what God is telling us there, as well as applying that truth to our daily Christian lives.

We want this series of books to grow into a basic library for every Christian, covering all the important topics and issues of the Christian life in an accessible, straightforward way. Currently the series includes books on holiness, encouragement, prayer, guidance, and defending the gospel.

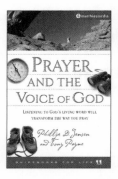 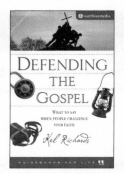 

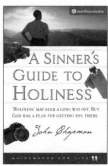 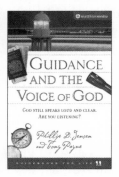

FOR MORE INFORMATION OR TO ORDER CONTACT:

Matthias Media
Telephone: +61-2-9663-1478
Facsimile: +61-2-9663-3265
Email: info@matthiasmedia.com.au
Internet: www.matthiasmedia.com.au

Matthias Media (USA)
Telephone: 1-866-407-4530
Facsimile: 724-498-1658
Email: sales@matthiasmedia.com
Internet: www.matthiasmedia.com

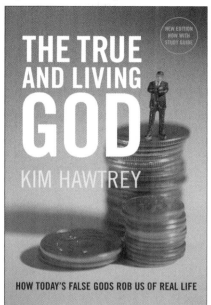

Stirrings of the Soul

By Michael Raiter

The explosion of interest in spirituality in our society is nothing short of phenomenal. New Age, feminist, environmental, occult, animal, vegetable and mineral ... While 'religion' and 'Christianity' arouse little enthusiasm from a disinterested and cynical public, 'spirituality' draws a crowd.

Among Christians, too, there is a flourishing interest in developing a greater 'spirituality'. Many who love the Lord Jesus Christ and long to please him seem frustrated that their spiritual lives—and the church services they attend—are too often dry and lacking in vitality. There has been a turn to the charismatic movement, to forms of mysticism, and even monasticism, in search of a way to 'practise the presence of God'.

In this intriguing and appealing book, Michael Raiter surveys contemporary spiritualities, highlighting both their enormous variety and their common features, and tracing their historical, cultural and social roots. He then addresses a range of important questions for Christians: What is true spirituality? If we were to meet a 'truly spiritual' person, what would he or she look like? How do we respond biblically to our longing for spiritual intimacy? And is evangelicalism, in its current expressions, contributing to an atmosphere of spiritual dryness?

FOR MORE INFORMATION OR TO ORDER CONTACT:

Matthias Media
Telephone: +61-2-9663-1478
Facsimile: +61-2-9663-3265
Email: info@matthiasmedia.com.au
Internet: www.matthiasmedia.com.au

Matthias Media (USA)
Telephone: 1-866-407-4530
Facsimile: 724-498-1658
Email: sales@matthiasmedia.com
Internet: www.matthiasmedia.com

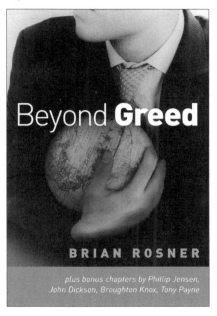